Essential Steps

Essential Steps

Scoping Custom Web and Mobile Projects

Thomas Smart

PARTRIDGE

Copyright © 2017 by Thomas Smart.

ISBN:	Hardcover	978-1-5437-4182-7
	Softcover	978-1-5437-4181-0
	eBook	978-1-5437-4195-7

All rights reserved. No part of this book may be used or reproduced by any means, graphic, electronic, or mechanical, including photocopying, recording, taping or by any information storage retrieval system without the written permission of the author except in the case of brief quotations embodied in critical articles and reviews.

Because of the dynamic nature of the Internet, any web addresses or links contained in this book may have changed since publication and may no longer be valid. The views expressed in this work are solely those of the author and do not necessarily reflect the views of the publisher, and the publisher hereby disclaims any responsibility for them.

Print information available on the last page.

To order additional copies of this book, contact
Toll Free 800 101 2657 (Singapore)
Toll Free 1 800 81 7340 (Malaysia)
orders.singapore@partridgepublishing.com

www.partridgepublishing.com/singapore

CONTENTS

About the Author vi
Acknowledgements vii
Preface ix
Prologue x

1. Analysis and Pain Points 1
2. Methodologies and Stakeholders 13
3. Kick-Off with a Strategy Session 22
4. Concept Validation and Competitor Analysis 29
5. User Requirements Validation 38
6. Realistic Approach to Budgeting 46
7. Planning a Marketing Strategy 51
8. Choosing the Right Platform and Technologies 57
9. Project Team Types Compared 70
10. Recruiting an In-House Team 77
11. Hiring Third-Party Vendors 85
12. Risk Margin Assessment 99
13. Technical Research & Wireframing 113
14. Solution Architecture 120

Epilogue 123
Appendix: Scoping Template 125

About the Author

Thomas Smart has been actively involved with digital projects for 14 years (at the time of writing) and has a passion for both efficiency and ideation.

His experience crosses all types and sizes of businesses and sectors, giving him a huge scope of expertise to draw upon when working on project scoping and risk mitigation for custom web and mobile applications. His approach draws upon a variety of different methodologies, enabling him to create strategies which work for both startups and multinational corporations (MNC).

Thomas has worked for global banks, major advertising agencies and hotels, as well as tech and medical startups. He joined Lloyds Register in 2017 to lead a new Data & Digital team in delivering projects and inspiring and facilitating an Agile mindset change across the organization.

Acknowledgements

Writing *Essential Steps* has been on my 'To Do' list for quite some time, but it seemed that as soon as I started writing I would get derailed by work and personal matters. That all changed when I met copywriter Karyn Lim, who provided much needed motivation and support in writing this book. So thank you, Karyn: without you this book would likely not exist!

Many thanks to Mary (word-service.com) who helped with editing and improving the language and grammar of the contents, and to Amna Zeeshan who designed the content visuals.

A big thank you to my wife, Meiting, whose tolerance and patience with me knows almost no bounds; and to my little boy, Blaze, who has given me a fresh perspective on many things.

Preface

It is widely acknowledged that custom software development projects often go over budget and deadlines are missed. This is the case in a wide range of businesses, from startups to MNCs, and across almost every industry.

What is not always clear is **why** budgets and timelines aren't met. The parties involved are quick to point a finger at each other and, once the project is over, relationships are often too fractured for a polite discussion about what went wrong. This lack of mutual evaluation and communication after failed projects is, more than likely, one of the main reasons these problems still exist.

In this book, I describe the essential steps you can implement to help reduce the chance of this happening on your own projects. While the steps themselves vary in complexity and involve techniques taken from Agile and other methodologies, they are explained in a way that's easy to understand, with minimal jargon and using relatable examples.

I will cover each essential step later in the book; but first, let me start with a familiar story. While fictional, this tale is a textbook business case drawn from my own experience as well as that of my clients and partners over the years.

The story begins in the summer of 2009 with a toy manufacturing company that has survived the financial crisis of 2008, and is looking to go digital to improve sales and business resilience.

Prologue

1 May 2009, Friday. 8.20am.

A slight sheen of sweat covers Mark's forehead as he steps, with great relief, into an air-conditioned office lobby. The summer heat is arriving and Mark feels stifled and out of place in his business suit on a 'casual' Friday. Still, for a meeting with the CEO, he isn't going to show up in a T-shirt.

Without lifting his head from his phone, Mark makes a beeline for the lift lobby while pulling up yesterday's email on the screen: "See me tomorrow at 8.30am in my office." Despite his careful scrutiny, there is no clue about this morning's agenda to be found - which leaves him uncomfortably in the dark.

It's 8.32am by the time Mark knocks on the office door of Mr Stephen Watts, CEO of Trusted Toys Company Inc, or 'TTC' for short. Through the frosted glass panel, Mark can make out the large frame of his boss leaning back in a chair as he calls him in.

"Good morning Mr Watts."

"Morning Mark, take a seat. How are things wrapping up with the Biz E-Track project?"

The Biz E-Track project is a dashboard program that processes data from different departments and turns them into easy-to-understand graphs and business reports. Mark has been the lead project manager and, if Mr. Watts' grin is anything to go by, senior management's vocal praise for the project has made its way up to the CEO.

"The final vendor payment just went out yesterday. Overall, the project has been on time and on budget."

"Great to hear! Now... let's talk about your next project."

Mr Watts pauses, looking Mark in the eye before continuing. "It will be the biggest change for TTC since our overseas expansion and I want you to be the project owner."

Mark nods calmly, even as his heart starts racing.

"Looking at the Biz E-Track project, you clearly have the skills to handle technology projects, and I heard you did well talking to the different departments and meeting their requirements," says Mr Watts. "I believe that taking on this project is the natural next step for you, and your career."

Mark can't help his growing excitement as he listens. It sounds like a big step closer to a promotion. Mr Watts himself seems equally excited, with his eyes practically gleaming when he gets to the potential of such a project.

"A digital transformation! Bringing TTC into the online age with an innovative and exciting eCommerce experience for our customers. What do you think about it?"

"Sounds great," Mark eagerly jumps in. "There are a number of ready-to-use eCommerce services we could use..."

Mr Watts cuts him off with a quick wave of his hand.

"Not likely, Mark. I have looked at a few of our competitors and they all have the same approach, standard eCommerce services that are carbon copies of one another."

Mr Watts clasps his hands and speaks with a firm conviction in his voice.

"I believe TTC should be a leader in this area and make something that truly stands out from the crowd. An innovative eCommerce website and mobile app for the uPhone."

"Considering the importance of this project to us, I have a target budget of 120k in mind - bigger than what you have worked with so far," he adds. "It would be great to launch this by the end of November. Christmas would be right around the corner - perfect timing! Seven months from now, would you say that is enough time?"

"I understand, sir. A custom built solution within 120k and seven months sounds feasible." Mark carefully words his reply. It's never a good idea to over-promise. "I will work on a proposal to confirm that."

"I trust you'll do it well."

Without a pause, Mark responds. "Thank you, Mr Watts. I'll get started straight away."

Jim from Operations is already leaning against his desk with an extra cup of coffee when Mark gets back. Jim is Mark's go-to man in the company, whether for coffee breaks or advice.

Mark grins as he takes the coffee. "Thanks, Jim."

"Well, you look happy. What's the word from the big boss? You get promoted finally?"

"Nothing about a promotion yet, but the boss has a new project for me - an eCommerce platform to sell our products."

"Wow! That's big, kinda like Amazing Inc.?"

Mark laughs. "Probably not that big, it's much simpler than that. Just a website and mobile app for customers to preview the toys, add to basket, checkout, that kind of thing."

"Doesn't sound easy. I heard a lot about these tech projects, they always go over budget like crazy."

"Maybe, but I have a pretty good budget and enough time. If I get started fast, there shouldn't be an issue."

As he begins thinking strategically about the project, it dawns on Mark that he isn't entirely sure how to manage a fully-custom project. On his last project, the requirements were given to him with an example set of reports as the expected result. Sourcing for an enterprise statistics software vendor was easy enough, and he quickly settled on an existing product recommended by one of TTC's distributors. It turned out to be a great fit for TTC's needs and, considering the licensing costs, the vendor was more than happy to help with a few customizations for some of the more complex reports that Finance required.

A custom project shouldn't be too different... Mark thinks as he Googled "custom ecommerce development". Scrolling through the results, he frowns. *No concrete template for a project management approach.* He comes across ads for eCommerce software products and an article about Agile SCRUM project management, but that doesn't seem relevant to a traditional enterprise like TTC.

Pushing back from his desk, Mark catches sight of Hassan installing a new computer two cubicles away. If Mark remembers correctly, Hassan transferred to TTC from a tech startup a year ago. *Not the easiest guy to talk to but he might have some advice for this project*, Mark thinks, and walks over.

Hassan perpetually has a troubled look on his face, even during lunch, and he is always in a rush to finish work. It seems the IT department is undergoing quite a turnover, and Hassan's brows furrow deeper as Mark comes over.

"Hey Hassan, haven't seen you on this floor for a while."

"Management has been keeping me busy upgrading the boardroom A/V. You need help with anything while I'm here?"

"Not exactly. Just wanted to grab you for a few minutes, and hear what you know about custom web and app development."

"Development?" Hassan's brows unfurrow as he realises Mark didn't have 'technical issues'. "I don't know much, beyond Windows scripting anyway."

"Maybe you know where to start? It's an eCommerce platform, a new project I'm overseeing."

"Huh, eCommerce. Easiest is off-the-shelf. Plenty available, *LargeCart* for example."

"We're going for a custom built solution…"

"Why?" Hassan raises an eyebrow at Mark.

"Well, senior management wants something unique that will stand out in the market. It's got to be custom built."

"Too risky. Off-the-shelf products are easier. You'd probably find something that would work."

"Sorry Hassan, but I have to agree with management that custom is the way to go if we want to make it big."

"Hm. Better leave it to developers then. Figure out your app's features, and leave the technical implementation to the experts." There is a tinge of disapproval in Hassan's words.

"Thanks, I appreciate the advice."

"If you're not careful, custom development will cost a lot more than you expect," Hassan's parting words sound ominously final.

Mark mentally brushes Hassan's concerns aside - he knows that such a project is risky, but the opportunity far outweighs the risks. A plan starts to form in Mark's mind as he leaves Hassan to his work. *Gather user requirements, find a vendor with a decent portfolio, get an estimate, and let the vendor implement it while keeping them on track with the timeline and budget.* A fairly simple plan, he just needs to get the requirements documented quickly so that enough time remains for development, with some room for any delays.

Susan from Marketing probably knows a development agency, and I can get her requirements for the project while I'm there, Mark thinks as he heads down to where Marketing, PR and Design are housed.

With all the creatives of TTC together, Floor 5 has its own unique look. Toys, posters, designs, and magazines are strewn everywhere like colourful decorations. They also take 'casual Friday' seriously, making Mark stand out like a sore thumb in his business attire as he walks across the floor. Ignoring the sideway glances from several designers, Mark looks around for Susan.

"Mark! Forgot that it's Friday?" Susan's loud, singsong voice comes from behind him.

Turning around, Mark sees Susan walking towards him in a flowing pastel dress which reaches her ankles. *Boho-chic now,* Mark mentally notes the latest fashion trend she has embraced.

"How could I forget?" Mark gasps in mock horror. "I was just looking for you." Susan is the director of Marketing and, though Mark's senior in age and position, they have become friendly after working on a few projects together.

"Lucky for you, I'm free right now. What can I do for you, Mr Mark?" Susan replies in jest, as walks towards her office with Mark in tow.

Mark laughed. "It's about a new project, for an eCommerce app…"

"Digital transformation, right?" Susan interjects, nodding at Mark to take a seat. "Stephen sent an email about it to the directors. It's a big one, congrats! Must have been the good job you did on the Biz E-Track project." Susan smiles.

"Thanks, Susan," Mark replies warmly, pleased with the praise.

"So, what do you need me for? Marketing campaign for the big launch?" Susan takes out a pen, twirling it in her hand.

"Definitely, we will need to work on that. How much would you say the campaign needs?"

"We could lower the total a bit by keeping design in-house and having our interns do some of the prep work." Susan starts scribbling notes and numbers on a loose sheet of paper as she speaks. "I'd say that 30k for external resources and ad budget should cover it. You can never have too much marketing budget though!"

"Alright. I'll put 30k aside in my budget for now," Mark assures her. "Also, I was wondering if you have any development vendors to recommend?"

"Hm…" Susan pauses to think. "There's the one that did up our website."

The website in question was a simple homepage for TTC with basic information on the company and products.

"They were alright, we did the design ourselves but they implemented the project on time and on budget. I'll send you their contact."

"That would be great," Mark says. "If it's not too much to ask, there's one more thing I could use your help with…"

Susan laughs as Mark's voice trails off. "Oh, don't be so polite. Shoot!"

Mark grins at her bluntness. It was one reason why working with Susan is easy.

"I'm thinking of a survey for the app. You know, get to know what customers want. Is there a mailing list of our customers I could use?"

"We don't keep one," says Susan with an apologetic shrug. "I could get my assistant to compile the contacts of distributors we work with, if that helps?"

"Sure, that might work! Thanks so much."

"You owe me one, Mark!" Susan adds in her singsong voice.

"If there's anything you want in the app, I'll do my best," jokes Mark. "While I'm here, might as well ask if you have any ideas so far?"

Susan sighs dramatically. "I haven't had time to think of many. But I do have one interesting idea…"

"Susan wants a puzzle game in the app.."

Seeing Jim's face, Mark explains. "…so users can solve and share puzzles through Facebook for credits. It's cool but…" Mark's shoulders slump slightly as he goes back to his lunch.

"Not really what the app needs to sell products?" Jim muses.

"Yeah but it is great for marketing. There shouldn't be a problem adding it in." Mark nods to himself, reassuringly. "Other directors heard about the project too, and I'm starting to get emails about their ideas…"

"The app is supposed to be for customers, right?" Jim asks, as he taps his fingers on the table. Mark can tell Jim is worried whenever he starts this unconscious habit.

"Right, but the directors are stakeholders as well and the app is owned by the company. They have some good ideas."

"I guess so. By the way, my boss wanted to talk to you about the app soon. He might have some good ideas too." Jim laughs, lightening the mood.

Truthfully, for every good idea, there are questionable ones. For example, Shawn, director of Operations, has a reasonable request to use their existing inventory system for the app which would avoid managing content in 2 different systems. But he also asks if Mark could include location tracking of mobile users when making a purchase with a live map for internal review.

Agreeing to some ideas and rejecting others risks upsetting some directors, and so, Mark diplomatically emails back and forth until a consensus is reached. Given that Michelle, director of Finance, is equally interested in tracking customers and their purchasing habits, Mark decides to satisfy both stakeholders by keeping the location tracking feature, though without the 'live' map which seems questionable in terms of privacy.

18 May, Monday.

Two weeks into the project and Mark finally finishes gathering requirements from stakeholders. With Susan's help, he sent out a short survey to over 150 distributors asking for their opinions on a new eCommerce app.

Only 18 responses have come back. Open-ended questions like "What makes a good eCommerce app?" elicit a variety of answers, some of which are clearly unhelpful. Survey 23's answer of "An app that sells products" came to mind. A couple of respondents take the time to give detailed answers; mostly they recommended a user-friendly interface, which still doesn't tell Mark much. Looking at the most popular eCommerce platforms is more useful, as he notes similar features like one-click shopping and detailed search functions.

Putting everything together, Mark ends up with 20 pages of requirements. Some features are well-detailed, such as the checkout workflow that Mark has written up himself after studying a few well-known eCommerce platforms. Others, like the inventory system, are left as high-level descriptions that Mark figures the developers will narrow down when work starts. The list includes all features which the stakeholders agree on, and Mark feels a deep sense of relief as he labels the document "Final requirements".

Finding a development vendor comes next. With limited digital presence, except for a plain website and their Facebook page, TTC has no contacts with development agencies that Mark can tap on besides the one Susan recommended. They get back to Mark with the disappointing news that they don't do such large-scale custom projects. However, they do suggest a website Mark could use to find other agencies: dlance.com.

After creating a new dlance.com account, Mark posts a generic summary brief for a custom eCommerce website and mobile app. He indicates in the brief that he only wants to work with local businesses as he feels that being able to have face-to-face meetings will make it easier for him to manage the project.

The following day, he starts to receive estimates starting from $30,000 - well below his budget. *If development costs so little, I'll have plenty leftover for additional marketing,* Mark happily thinks to himself. He shortlists five agencies based on their portfolio experience with eCommerce, and arranges meetings with each of them to give them the full brief.

As he prepares for the first meeting, Hassan's parting warning comes to mind and Mark decides to play it safe by omitting his budget from the brief. *Sharing the budget upfront will only let developers know how much they **could** charge*, he thinks.

---

27 May, Wednesday.

Finally, the last meeting. Mark's mind drifts from the presentation before him. This is the last agency he has to meet, and as he has come to expect after the other four presentations, they have sent a lead developer and a well-prepared salesperson armed with an impressive slide deck to his office. And, as usual, they pitch **their** approach and technology as the best one for the TTC eCommerce project.

"... we have a fully AGILE capable team, which gives you the best project management method in the industry right now. With our excellent testing capabilities, you can rest assured that you will have a fully-functional, high-quality app at the end." The young lady beams with confidence as she concludes her sales pitch.

"Any questions?" She looks expectantly at her audience. Mark shakes his head with a smile. As he stands up to thank her, exchanging small talk, he inwardly sighs. *They all sound the same.*

One development agency was highly experienced in *GrammarPress*, an existing stable platform that the salesperson swore would not fail and could be fully customized into a unique solution. Another recommended that customizing an existing eCommerce platform, *Gamento*, would be the best approach, and promised that it would "fit all your eCommerce needs both for the users and the admins". The remaining agencies proposed a custom built solution based on various programming languages with which they had the most experience.

Without much technical knowledge, Mark bases his evaluation partly on how well he can get along with the lead developer. It is crucial that he gets on with the developers if he is to manage them well. The agency that seems the most promising has a lead developer who is very open to the ideas in the requirements document, and easy to talk to. Other lead developers asked repetitive questions - the same query phrased in different ways - which leaves him feeling they are a bit slow to understand what he needs. Most important, though, is the updated estimate he asks each agency to provide in their proposal after they have been given the full project brief.

---

1 June, Monday.

The week after the last meeting, all the final estimates are in.

$40,000 is the lowest offer, from the agency who pitched *GrammarPress*. Following it are three estimates in the mid-range of $60,000 to $75,000. And finally, the highest quote of $105,000 from a young agency recommending a custom built solution on a new hosting service provided by 'Amazing Inc.' - a major eCommerce player itself.

The cost is unsurprising. Their lead developer has cautioned Mark that it costs more to develop for a new platform that, "automatically grows with the number of visitors," but, "the benefits are worth it," as their business developer has mentioned more than once. Mark also notes that they have included four weeks of research and six weeks of testing which places it dangerously close to the final deadline.

Given his budget of $90,000 after marketing costs and the closeness to the final deadline of the proposed schedule, Mark crosses out the last option immediately. He also doubts the need for so much research and testing, or for a platform that "automatically grows". From what he understands, regular hosting services can support tens of thousands of users, which seems more than enough for TTC's needs.

The cheapest estimate is crossed out, too, as a cautionary measure against what seems to be underpriced compared to the other solutions. This leaves Mark with the three mid-range choices, which cost more than initial estimates, but are still well within budget.

With similar cost proposals and indistinguishable sales pitches, Mark's final decision comes down to his personal impression of the three agencies. Fortunately, the lead developer Mark likes is from one of them, and, while the highest one of the three, their estimate of $75,000 fits nicely within his budget. Their proposed timeline is one month of design, three months of development and one week of testing. This means that development could finish almost two months ahead of time if they start soon. *It seems my choice is made,* Mark thinks as he picks out their business card.

> Adam Steele
> **Lead developer**
> *Wired Labs*

---

3 June, Wednesday. 2.55pm.

Nervous excitement courses through Mark as he knocks on the boardroom door. He is about to present a complete project proposal to the CEO, who is already in the boardroom after a previous meeting.

"Come in," Mr Watt's muffled voice comes through the glass. Mark nervously adjusts his tie before pushing the door open. "Good afternoon, Mr Watts."

"Afternoon Mark, let's get started. Run me through the brief please." The documents are already laid out in front of Mr Watts.

While setting up his presentation slides, he thinks about the project's progress. *Everything has gone according to plan so far. All I need is this approval.*

"With a custom built web and mobile app, the eCommerce project will take TTC through a **digital transformation**," Mark starts. He catches Mr Watts' slight smile at the use of his catchphrase - *a good sign*. "To make something that stands out, our app will have custom features not found in the current market…

"Marketing gave their requirement for a puzzle builder feature that will be used in social media marketing," explains Mark as a mock-up visual, which he had gotten from Marketing, comes up on screen. Mr Watts smiles approvingly when he sees this. *Thank you Susan!*

"Operations requested that the app use their existing inventory system. This should save us thousands of dollars in development and allow operations to manage the inventory in only one system."

In this manner, Mark goes through the summarized user requirements. He breathes a sigh of relief internally as Mr Watts nods along. Negotiating six directors' demands have not been an easy task and compiling everything into a coherent summary was an equally challenging feat. Mark cannot be happier with the CEO's apparent approval.

The rest of the presentation passes without a hitch. Mr Watts seems impressed when Mark introduces the development vendor, *Wired Labs*, with a few tech buzzwords picked up from their sales pitch - "AGILE team", "interactive UX design", "a focus on application security".

"Their estimated timeline is four months of design and development. If we start next week, it should be finished by the start of October." Mark summarizes.

"So, the launch will be ready by December?" Mr Watts asks seriously, as the presentation comes to an end.

"Yes sir. We would be weeks ahead of schedule, so there is enough buffer even if unexpected delays occur."

Mr Watts grins, and shuffles through the brief documents. "I see that you are within budget as well," Mr Watts says, as he pulls out a page and scans through the numbers at the bottom.

Mark responds modestly. "Yes, though development might end up costing more than the estimate, but I'm quite sure the excess 15k can cover any additional costs."

"Seems like you have everything under control," chuckles Mr Watts. *He's going to approve it,* thinks Mark.

"Just one thing... it says here," Mr Watts' finger traces a section of the document, "that development will start with the web app."

"That's right, sir." Mark confirms. "As proposed by Wired Labs".

"Start with the uPhone app first. I talked to people about this idea - some of them are big in the eCommerce industry, you know - and mobile is the way to go. It's better to focus on mobile as that will be most important, web can come after."

Mark pauses to think about this. *It's just rearranging the order, there shouldn't be an issue.* "I will ask the development vendor to adjust their schedule accordingly, sir."

"Great, go ahead and get started then." Mr Watts grins, as he signs the proposal.

"Thank you, sir!" Mark replies enthusiastically.

Naturally, Adam, the lead developer of *Wired Labs,* is excited about the big deal. Mark can picture Adam jumping out of his chair from the excitement in his voice over the phone.

"That's amazing! Thank you, Mark, it's a great opportunity to work together."

"I look forward to it as well." Mark says sincerely. He is glad to work with someone he gets along with.

"Oh, there is one small change to the schedule after talking to the CEO. We need to start developing the uPhone app before the website." Mark says, bringing up Mr Watt's request.

"Eh- erm…" Adam's hesitance was clear. "It's always easier and faster to iterate in a web app first. It takes longer to implement changes in mobile, and it costs more than web changes."

"Right, but either way, both have to be developed. The CEO is quite insistent on mobile first," says Mark.

"If you are sure about it… I'll let the team know."

"Thanks Adam, go ahead." *There's enough budget for changes*, Mark reassures himself.

"This changes our schedule a bit, but we'll still start with the design wireframes. When design is done, we can move onto the API and start building the app in parallel." Adam explains. "I'll be updating you on the progress every two weeks, does that work?"

"Sure, can we get started this week?" Mark asks eagerly.

"Sorry, we can't start until Monday the week after," Adam' replies apologetically.

"How come?" Mark has assumed they could start anytime.

"We are still finishing up another project and some of our developers are on leave - it's school holiday, gotta take the kids out," Adam lightheartedly says by way of explanation.

Mark laughs politely while checking his calendar, "Alright then, we start 15th of June."

Ending the call with Adam, Mark recounts the timeline with the milestones Adam had mentioned. *Design should be done by 13 July, development by 5 October, and after testing is done, we finish by 12 October.* Mark marks the dates in his calendar. *Still ahead of the deadline.*

15 June, Monday.

"T-minus 16 weeks!" is the enthusiastic title of Adam's email marking the start of the project. Over his first cup of coffee, Mark smiles and eagerly reads through the contents.

In his email, Adam mentions that the team will follow TTC's corporate branding guidelines, and "found good inspiration" from the two eCommerce sites that Mark had provided as reference. Adam also assures Mark that the wireframes are underway and will be done in two weeks. Feeling pleased, Mark quickly replies, giving Adam the go-ahead.

26 June, Friday.

Mark scans through the wireframes of the app's main pages - Home, Products, Search, Product Details, and Shopping Cart. There has been little contact with Adam over the last two weeks, apart from a few emails confirming design and content details, but it seems like there were no issues and the results were received on schedule.

Scrolling through the black-and-white outlines is not very inspiring, but it does give him a sense of the app's general flow and keeps him focused on functionality. *Great to see all the features we scoped, they look like they will work well together,* he mulls to himself.

No need to hold a stakeholder meeting just for these wireframes, Mark decides in the interest of efficiency. He carefully crafts an email asking for feedback, sneaking in a mention that the full designs are in progress to manage expectations, before forwarding the wireframes to the directors.

Over the course of the day, responses come in. Most of them are along the line of agreement and "looking forward to the final designs". Unsurprisingly, Susan has the most comments about the position and size of various elements, and suggestions for "suitable colours". Francis from the legal team has asked for a disclaimer at the bottom of the page. *Should be fairly straightforward,* Mark thinks.

By the end of the day, Mark sends the feedback to Adam, and receives a reply the following Monday that the team can easily make the changes. The first draft design proposals for key pages are sent to Mark later on in the week, and are quickly approved by the stakeholders.

10 July, Friday.

Four weeks after the kick-off and the full set of design proposals are in. At first glance, they look great - eye-catching, sleek, and most importantly, unique - at least, to Mark. Hoping that the other stakeholders felt the same, Mark forwards the designs.

This time round, there are a lot more comments and change requests. While Mr Watts is impressed with the look of it, not all the directors are on board. After some back-and-forth discussions, Mark realizes that more changes are needed. One of them is the previously approved Home page design, with a few directors agreeing that the underlying News page should be added to it.

"Sure," Adam says confidently over the phone, "the changes are minor, so each one should only take about a day or two. Send me the list and I'll get a total estimate for you, Mark."

"Thanks Adam, that's a big help." Mark is relieved. He has called Adam to run over the new issues and find out how long it would take to fix them.

In the end, Adam concludes that two weeks are needed to finish up the design changes after reviewing the change requests. More than Mark expected, but well within the timeline. *We'll still be ahead of schedule,* Mark thought as he edited his previous schedule. *Development done by 19 October, and testing by 26 October.*

24 July, Friday.

With the final designs completed in a timely fashion, the approval goes smoothly. Holding a stakeholder meeting with the CEO and directors present, Mark reviews the changes and receives warm praise from Mr Watts himself.

"It's great that you listened to everyone, Mark, it looks better than I could imagine!" Mr Watts enthuses at the end of the meeting. From there, the remaining stakeholders give their sign-offs easily.

But Adam brings bad news to the table when Mark gets on a call with him.

"Mark, the final designs increased the scope," Adam speaks slowly. *Less confident than before,* Mark notes.

"On the bright side, it did clear up some unclear requirements," Adam's voice picks up slightly, "but now we know that they'll take more time to complete."

"There was an issue with the requirements?" Mark probes. Why *didn't I hear about this before.*

"Well, there is always some uncertainty at the start of custom projects," Adam quickly replies, "and the extra changes introduced new requirements that bumped up the estimate too."

"Hmm, I see. How much longer are we looking at?"

"Three weeks more of development, to be safe."

Mark mentally calculates the new timeline. "We'll be done in the second week of November then?"

"If there aren't more changes, it's doable!" Adam assures him.

The new timeline will cut it much closer to the deadline of December, and Mark can't help but worry that things aren't going as smoothly as before.

Development starts immediately the following Monday, with Mark urging Adam to keep on task with the deliverables.

7 August, Friday.

At the end of the first two weeks of development, Adam presents the mostly completed API that the app will need. Mark doesn't know much about the technical jargon and is not able to verify the API as it requires programming capabilities to use, but is happy to know that it is going according to plan.

21 August, Friday.

The next update hits a snag. The first draft of the mobile landing page is ready for use, which gives Mark something concrete to mark progress. However, Adam informs Mark that one of its features doesn't implement as expected in mobile: it is causing problems with two other key features, and it will take another week to find an alternative.

It seems obvious to Mark that the developers are taking too long to fix things, but Adam defends his team. "It takes three times the work to change things on mobile - what takes a day in web takes three in mobile."

Without a quick solution, Mark can only take Adam's word for it and add another week to his timeline. The new estimated completion date is now 23 November.

4 September, Friday.

As the draft app deliverables flow in, page by page, Mark and the stakeholders get a first-hand taste of the app working on their phones. But tablets are a different story.

One of the directors tries out the app on her uPad, only to find that the pages look stretched out and not all the features are where they are supposed to be. She raises the issue to Mark, with Mr Watts CC-ed into the loop as well, and Mr Watts follows up with his own email stating the importance of the app working on **BOTH** mobile phones and tablets. Mark groans aloud at the messy interface as he dials Adam's number.

"The tablet requirement wasn't specified in the brief..." Adam rebuts defensively as soon as he hears the news.

"If we are making a mobile app, shouldn't it work on the uPhone AND uPad?" Mark snipes back. "Anyway, it has to be fixed. The CEO isn't happy with this."

Adam doesn't reply immediately, and when he does, he sounds uncharacteristically cheerless.

"We can make some design and code changes so that it looks fine on tablet, but this adds another week of development."

"Can't it be done any faster? We are hitting our deadline at this rate."

"We are working on it as fast as we can, but it needs at least a week to be done right." Adam insists.

"... Alright, send me the updated estimates today," Mark says sternly.

The new timeline and cost estimate that comes at the end of the day leaves Mark dejected. 30 November is the projected completion date and the cost estimate has been bumped up to $85,000. *$5,000 shy of blowing the budget. Any more delays and I will have a difficult time explaining this to Mr Watts.*

16 September, Wednesday.

It is mid-way through the project when Susan drops Mark an email asking to meet to discuss the app. Heading down to her office, Mark hopes that it is about the post-launch marketing.

"Mark! How's the app?" Susan asks cheerfully when Mark walks in.

"We're meeting our targets. You wanted to talk about it?" Mark tries to sound cheerful and avoid more questions.

"Right, it's the puzzle builder feature," Susan gets straight to the point and opens the working-version app on her phone. "I love how it looks, but there are some issues."

Mark nods for her to continue while groaning inwardly.

"None of my product images are working, it shows me an error saying that it is either the wrong file type or the dimensions are too large. I had assumed that a feature as standard as an image upload would work the same as most popular sites these days, with the image being resized or converted by the application. This is just a very bad user experience and it will be very difficult for mobile users to submit images as the default camera photos are also too large." She points to her screen as the puzzle builder page shows up.

Susan goes on to elaborate specifically about what exactly she wants in the feature - which makes sense to Mark now, though it wasn't mentioned in the previous requirements.

"It's really important that we get this feature right, what do you say, Mark?" Susan looks expectantly at Mark.

"At this stage… I don't think we can entertain any more changes," Mark mutters nervously as he sees Susan frowning.

"What do you mean?" Susan raises her voice. She is as straightforward as ever and Mark can envisage the uphill battle ahead.

"We're barely keeping to the timeline and budget right now. Any more changes and we won't make it."

"There's got to be a way. If it doesn't get fixed, the feature is almost useless!" Susan impatiently exits the app as she speaks, emphasising her point.

Mark fidgets in his seat. The desk plate on the table stares him in the face like a silent threat - "Susan Ang, Director of Marketing". Susan will win this round, and he eventually agrees to her requests, hoping for a solution from the developers.

"It's unfortunate, but if we started with web, it would be done in a day," Adam says when Mark calls him. Despite the carefully measured tone, Mark can pick up a hint of annoyance behind Adam's words. "It needs a week more."

Things have been going from bad to worse. With Adam's new projection, it has reached a definitive new low. Mark will need to ask Mr Watts to extend the deadline.

18 September, Friday.

Mr Watts is, understandably, not happy about the deadline extension to 7 December, but passes it without much comment after asking Mark to explain. It is still within an acceptable margin to release the app for the December sales, and so Mr Watts simply tells Mark to keep it on time.

2 October, Friday.

While the changes to the puzzle builder feature are worked on, Mark gets an update that 70% of the app is completed. He sighs and double-checks the requirements list. *Not much visible progress to show the stakeholders this week.*

16 October, Friday.

Mark paces the meeting room, waiting for Adam to arrive on the premises. This will be their first meeting since development started, and it does not bode well.

Adam called the day before with urgent news that development had hit a serious problem with the inventory which would be easier to explain in person. This meeting was the result, and Adam is running late.

When Adam turns up, ten minutes after the arranged time, there is palpable tension between the two men. Adam is visibly worn out, with dark rings around his eyes. The situation is notably different from a few months ago.

It takes 20 minutes for Adam to go through all the problems with the inventory system. Mark doesn't understand some technical points, but he does realise that it is a huge issue. TTC's existing inventory system is basically incompatible with the mobile app. It uses ten-year-old proprietary software, which means that data and access are encrypted and no third-party software can access it directly.

Adam mentions that they *could* manually export data and import it into the application, but this will require a lot of work to make the data structure compatible with the application before importing. Because the inventory system was never intended for public display of products, there are many records for 'internal circulation only'. These records should not be imported into the application, and it will require manual cleaning to ensure they are left out.

He ends by suggesting a best-option solution - a custom inventory system with a new interface and changes to the API. This meant 3 more weeks of development.

"Why wasn't this brought up earlier? Why am I only hearing about it now?" Mark gives up on maintaining their previous friendliness.

"We… we didn't know about these technology issues… with the project starting right away… and all the changes… there was no time to find out earlier." Adam is defensive, bursting with excuses, in Mark's view.

The meeting between the two ends uncomfortably, with Mark rushing off to talk to the Operations team. He needs to settle the issue as quickly as possible. It turns out that they are are not open to the idea. The Operations director demands to know who is going to cover the additional resources needed to work with two inventory systems.

But by far, Mr Watts is the angriest. The app won't be completed until the end of December and now exceeds the budget by $35,000. The hour-long budget approval session with Mr Watts, in which Mark's boss questions his project management, leaves him entirely demoralised.

"I am deeply disappointed by this, Mark. It is completely unacceptable." Mr Watts says. In that moment, the prospect of promotion disappears right before Mark's eyes.

30 October, Friday.

By now, Mark has taken it upon himself to video-call Adam weekly for updates to make sure there are no further issues. Adam insists that his team is working on the new inventory system as fast as they can. Rarely, though, do the conversations end without a barely-masked snide remark from Mark about the project's status.

27 November, Friday.

At the end of November - the project's initial due date - Adam reports that the mobile app is mostly completed and they will be starting on the eCommerce website. The news doesn't make Mark feel any better when the monthly invoice comes in.

18 December, Friday.

To Mark's great relief, no issues pop up for the website, and they reach the end of development. At this point, Mark cannot wait any longer and ponders the possibility of releasing the app without testing.

"Launching an app full of bugs is way worse than waiting one more week," Jim says wisely, when Mark mentions the idea to him over lunch.

"True…" Mark mulls over Jim's advice and decides against being hasty.

25 December, Friday.

It is Christmas Day, and Mark sits forlornly at his desk at home, staring at a screen with a long list of unread emails on it.

Jim's advice has turned out to be right. There are a ton of issues that turn up during testing. On top of that, Mark has released the beta version to all the stakeholders, with the expectation that they would be happy to see the final product.

While they were indeed excited, almost everyone has some minor things they want changing - from image sizes to the choice of words. The numerous change requests and bugs have been a mess to navigate, and Mark prepares himself for another round of tedious negotiations with Adam, on Christmas day no less. But with the project in its last stages, Mark wants this to be over. He sets up the video call with Adam.

"Hi Mark," Adam says unenthusiastically as his face pops up on the screen. "Merry Christmas."

That sounds sarcastic, Mark thinks, but brushes it aside. He returns the half-hearted greetings and gets to discussing the changes briskly. Adam remains silent until the end where he duly mentions the team needing another month.

"What?" Mark replies in disbelief.

"Some of our developers are on leave, Mark. It's the holidays." Adam says pointedly, and takes a deep breath before continuing.

"Every time we fix something, something else breaks. And the work doubles when you take into account we are working with mobile and web. With all these change requests, my team is facing a huge amount of pressure here. We have to debug a lot of the code with each change that we make..."

"The bugs aren't my problem, Adam," Mark, irritated, interrupts Adam's complaints. *None of this would have happened if you developed it right!*

"Another month is unacceptable. We might not go ahead with Wired Labs in the future with this performance." Mark puts his foot down.

"Hey, it isn't all our fault. The new inventory system completely changed the structure of the databases. We had to cut back on testing during development to meet the deadline, and our developers just didn't have the time to do the automated testing scripts." Adam looks like he is at the end of his patience, and so is Mark.

"That isn't the point now. I can't afford another month to fix a few bugs. I'll cut down on the change requests, and I want it done in 3 weeks."

"Fine, I'll pull some developers back but it'll cost more." Adam mutters reluctantly.

Mark hangs up shortly after, thinking morosely about how to break the news to Mr Watts.

4 January 2010, Monday.

The first working day of the New Year, and Mark starts it by facing Mr Watts' wrath in the office.

"A month over the deadline and now this! $60,000 over budget!" Mr Watts is red in the face and almost shouting. Mark knows for sure that anyone passing by Mr Watts' office can hear him.

The budget has gone up $25,000 from the last approval, and Mark mentally curses Adam for it. Overtime charges for developers cost much more than he has anticipated.

"Sir, there were a lot of problems with development… and we have to fix things for this app to work." Mark wishes he could be anywhere else as he tries to placate Mr Watts.

"This had better be the end of it. I want to see it up and running the next time I hear from you." Mr Watts shakes his head unhappily while signing off on the budget approval.

As Mark leaves the office, downcast, he can hear Mr Watts muttering angrily behind him.

"Who knows if this is worth it."

15 January 2010, Friday.

It was late at night that Mark receives a text from Adam that testing is done and the app is finished.

Even though it is finally over, Mark cannot find any relief in it. By now, all the directors know about his massive failure to keep to the deadline and budget.

Seven weeks over the deadline with a cost 150% of the original budget. *Nothing to boast about*, Mark thinks wryly. He types a curt thanks to Adam and the team, and heads to bed. It is the first good night's sleep he has had in a long time.

18 January 2010, Monday.

Monday marks the start of the marketing campaign for the app's release. It is Susan's job from here, and Mark passes over the baton gladly.

Mr Watts is significantly happier at the in-office launch party, but remains clearly distant from Mark throughout. During the congratulatory speech, he simply gives a nod in Mark's direction. The project's failure hangs heavily on Mark's heart as it sinks in that it is truly over.

Jim comes over to pat Mark on the back. "It's finally over, cheer up!"

"Yeah, I did my best." Mark tries to be optimistic. *It couldn't be helped that the developers messed everything up.*

1 March 2010, Monday.

Susan's marketing campaign is a total success. Over the past few months, great user reviews roll in one after the other, along with a hike in sales. TTC has reached a new level of global exposure as new customers are drawn in by the buzz on social media.

When Mr Watts calls Mark in for an after-action review of the project, he is much easier on Mark than before. It seems the app's success has partially redeemed Mark in his eyes. However, there is no mention of a promotion and Mark leaves the room disheartened.

I should be happy I still have my job, he tells himself as he takes out his phone, which he has silenced before the meeting. He is met with a string of missed calls lighting up his screen. His heart races as he scrolls through the list - Susan, Jim, IT, and even TTC's Customer Service have called. An email notification pops up as he holds the phone.

The subject: "[Urgent] Website and App down"

With his hands shaking, Mark skims over the email in a daze. There has been a surge of people using the app from Susan's most recent campaign, which went viral. The high traffic has crashed the server, which was unprepared for such numbers. The website, and API that the mobile app relies on, are both unreachable.

*"Fail to Plan;
Plan to Fail"*

1

Analysis and Pain Points

The pitfalls and pain points of the current situation should be recognizable after reading Mark's story. Most common is the problem of development going over deadlines and budgets, often to an almost astronomical extent. Similarly, the pain points of fixed price projects are deteriorating quality and debugging stages that seem to never end.

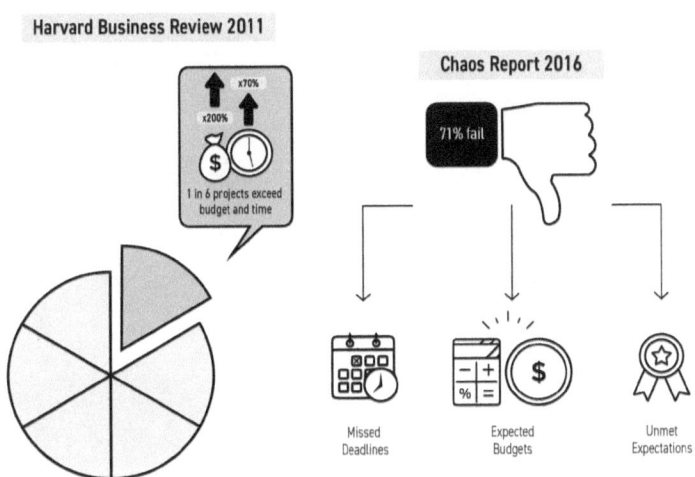

One in six IT projects goes over budget by 200% and takes 70% more time to complete than expected.

This is according to the largest global study of IT projects by Harvard Business Review (2011)* which compared project estimates against actual costs and results. Even more disheartening is the landmark study of IT project failure, the CHAOS Report (2015) by the Standish Group**, which found that **71% of digital projects will fail** - missing deadlines, budgets or quality expectations.

These statistics are not meant to deter you from embarking on your project, but to encourage you to learn from others' experiences to increase your chances of success.

Why did Mark's project fail to meet expectations? And was failure truly unavoidable?

The answer is that despite giving the project his full attention and having the best intentions at every step, Mark failed to sufficiently scope and research the project before development started. Many of the problems he encountered could have been mitigated, or at least, reduced if he had a better understanding of the industry and had done some additional preparations. Knowing where he went wrong and what could have been done might save you from a story like Mark's.

---

* https://hbr.org/2011/09/why-your-it-project-may-be-riskier-than-you-think

** https://www.infoq.com/articles/standish-chaos-2015

Mark — **Essential Steps**

> Asking stakeholders "what they want" without a clear structure, or a reason for each requirement.

> Discussion should be structured through goals - workflows - requirements. Requirements should be based on actual user needs and contribute to a goal or workflow.
> *Chapter 03*

> Accepting stakeholders' high-level requirements - such as the project being a custom implementation - without fact-checking or comparing alternatives.

> Stakeholders can provide their preferences but these and alternatives need to be researched and presented to ensure the final decision is based on fact.
> *Chapter 03,08*

> Basing costly business decisions on assumptions, without even minimal market research.

Mark   Essential Steps

> A project should be validated in the market and questions asked before too much resources are put into it. Is there a market need? Is the chosen implementation the best way to meet this need and the business goals? Is there a faster more affordable way to trial the idea before committing to a more costly version?
>
> *Chapter 04*

> Taking stakeholders' feature requirements without validating them with the actual users of the solution. While Mark did try to do a survey, the distributors were never the intended users of the project.user needs and contribute to a goal or workflow.

> All requirements should be validated with actual users to ensure this is a feature they need and that you have not missed anything essential to those users. You should be in contact with actual users and make efforts to understand their needs before you build something for them.
>
> *Chapter 05*

> Focusing on the development cost of a project and assigning the entire budget to this area.

Mark | Essential Steps

> Development is just a small part of a project. While Mark correctly budgeted for marketing, this is often skipped. Also keep the following in mind for the budget: design, training, project management, testing and debugging, plus margins for issues/changes/additions.
>
> *Chapter 06,07*

> Managing a custom development project without any technical experience.

> If you do not have a technical background then find someone to support you who does: either a colleague who has hands-on technical experience with custom projects, or an external consultant. The consultant should be an independent third party and not part of the vendor's team.
>
> *Chapter 03,09*

> Only open to using local vendors.

Mark — **Essential Steps**

> Not necessarily a bad approach as it will reduce the risk exposure, certainly for managers with no technical experience. But offshore vendors can cost significantly less and, if briefed and managed the right way, the additional risk can be mitigated and final cost reduced.
>
> *Chapter 09,11*

Letting the platform and technology be decided by the developers' experience.

> A project's platform and technology should be based on what is best for the project's users and its long-term goals. The developers should be picked for that technology, not the other way around.
>
> *Chapter 08*

Putting mobile development before web development.

Mark

> In projects that include both mobile and web development, it is recommended to start with the web version first. Web development costs about a third of mobile, so any iteration during development will be more expensive on mobile.
>
> *Chapter 08*

> Expecting development agencies to include consultancy or consider your requirements from a long term or business perspective.

> Developers have been largely commoditized. This limits services such as consultancy and research outside a specific technical scope. This is a result of the market picking developers based primarily on cost.
>
> *Chapter 09,10 & 11*

> Picking a developer based on their marketing pitch, how likeable they are, or (only) price.

Mark   **Essential Steps**

> A developer should be picked based on their experience, quality of work, and their development capabilities and processes (such as testing procedures). To assess this you must review the vendor in detail with technical or at least relevant operational knowledge. Price estimates in the current market are highly unreliable because development services have been commoditized.
>
> *Chapter 09, 10 & 11*

> Underestimating the time required for testing, or worse - pushing back on the developer's recommendation for testing time. One week of planned testing after three months of development is simply not enough.

> This also comes back to the commoditization of development vendors who tend to reduce testing time in their estimates to keep them lower - often expecting the client to do significant testing themselves. For custom projects you should have a **minimum** of 25% testing time both **during** (unit tests) and **after** development (quality assurance, external testing, UAT).
>
> *Chapter 10, 11*

Mark

> Not adding adequate risk margins to the estimated timeline and cost.

> Calculate and add risk margins to estimates that are appropriate for the specific project, stakeholders, and vendor. A generic flat percentage is useful for an initial indication or when working with a fixed budget, but to get a more accurate risk margin it is essential to look at each individual project's specific risk exposure.
>
> *Chapter 12*

> Ignoring technologies and different implementations (such as scaling) without looking at the facts and doing a fair comparison with other implementations across both cost and benefits.

> Vendors who recommend certain technologies should not be dismissed offhand. All reasonable implementations of your project should be explored with at least a minimum of factual research and comparison. Scaling infrastructure means that it can grow and shrink with the number of active users. It also means that there is no single point of failure. A broken server or too many users will not, therefore, cause your platform to go offline.
>
> *Chapter 08*

| Mark | Essential Steps |

> Jumping straight into development and iterating along the way despite unknowns, unanswered questions and research areas.

>> Answer open questions with technical research and wireframing before starting development. Assume there will always be changes during development, but research and answer all the major unknowns and risk areas beforehand to get a better idea of the scope and cost of the project.
>> *Chapter 13*

> Expecting developers to make high-level architectural decisions without a clear understanding of your business goals and long term project roadmap.

>> Decisions that can affect your business or your project's long term goals should be made before development starts and communicated to the developers so they can consider these when making technical decisions.
>> *Chapter 13*

Mark

> Requirements that leave too much room for interpretation.

> Requirements need to be briefed in sufficient detail to developers so that any misunderstandings are minimised. Single requirements with an estimate higher than a few hours should be broken down into smaller requirements.
>
> *Chapter 03,05*

"Understand and choose the right approach for your project and team"

2

Methodologies and Stakeholders

Before beginning the essential steps, it will help if you have at least a basic understanding of common project management methodologies, their strengths and their weaknesses. There are many ways to approach projects, but they mainly fall into the Waterfall, Agile and Iterative methods or variations thereof. Here is a simplified summary of these three methods:

1. Waterfall

This classic approach was first described in 1956 and is still in use by many Multinational Corporations (MNCs) today as it fits nicely with their budgeting and Purchase Order (PO) workflow. With the Waterfall method, all requirements are scoped upfront in complete detail and a fixed budget is assigned and accepted based on the estimate. Then, the project is implemented following the schedule to the letter, and finally tested. This works well with off-the-shelf (OTS) solutions that have fixed requirements and limited customization, but is less suitable for custom projects as it has very little flexibility and limited tolerance for unforeseen risks. This leads to a significant chance of budgets and timelines not being met due to the unpredictable nature of custom projects.

2. Agile

There is ongoing debate on what Agile actually is, but a particular variant called Scrum has become especially popular in web and mobile project management. In general, you scope the main requirements upfront, and start implementing, iterating and testing in weekly or bi-weekly cycles of deliverables. Agile rightly states that not all risks can be predicted, and its processes are better suited to custom development projects as it allows for early prediction of missed deadlines and budgets. However, the process seems more focused on predicting these issues than mitigating them. Agile is also difficult for MNCs to implement as it requires significant changes to their traditional workflows, flexible budget and timelines, frequent touch points and fast decisions.

3. Iterative

While Agile is also considered iterative, you can push that to an extreme. In Iterative development, there is almost no scoping upfront, and development starts as soon as possible with frequent iteration and experimentation. This is a preferred method of tech entrepreneurs who initially do development themselves, but it does not scale well. In a team context, it is great for producing prototypes quickly where quality is not a concern. Mistakes are expected and part of the discovery process. This makes the Iterative method highly unpredictable but quick to deliver something tangible.

The shortcomings of the three methodologies, along with factors like poor planning and communication, are the leading cause of many pain points in custom development projects.

Next, we will look at different types of stakeholders involved with custom development projects to understand their unique challenges.

1. Developers and development agencies

The common misunderstandings between developers and clients are typically caused by a technical knowledge gap or misaligned expectations.

To non-technical clients, developers' sales pitches have the same message and buzzwords. Most clients do not have the technical knowledge required to ask the right questions that delve into the inner workings of the business to better evaluate their quality and methodology. While bigger clients may have onboarding policies and detailed contracts binding vendors to responsibilities, these rarely have any benefit or consequence in a real-world project. Thus, the industry itself is now increasingly commoditized as clients resort to comparing vendors based primarily on price.

Commoditized developers competing on price are forced to cut corners if they are to continue winning projects. The first casualties are upfront planning and research. The developers focus on establishing a list of functional requirements without asking if each requirement actually has a Return On Investment (ROI). In addition, they will skip much of the in-depth technical research to determine exactly if and how complex requirements are to be implemented, leaving this to be decided during the development phase. Even when they do include some research, it is typically only focused on the immediate requirements, and rarely considers a multi-year roadmap. This lowers their initial estimate and the effort required to produce it, and it enables them to deliver the more tangible code results earlier in the project timeline.

One of the big issues here is that most clients still have the expectation of a partnership with the vendor which would include research and consultancy taking place. They may not be able to articulate this requirement, but it is still an assumption, and a dangerous one at that. The negative impact of this approach is that estimates are significantly lower than final project cost and very limited risk assessment and mitigation takes place. During development, the developer needs to make last-minute decisions on how to implement the task assigned to them. When there are frequent changes, consistency between developers breaks down and project components do not scale because they are developed for the current known situation instead of for the long-term roadmap.

I must to stress that we should not blame developers for this situation, as they are forced to compete on price to survive in the current market. In the industry, greater education is needed for clients to understand the work that should happen before development, in order for the project to have the best possible chance of success. Clients need to specify this to vendors as part of the brief, give voice to their expectations of appropriate consultancy and research and to allow developers to do technical research and detailed architecture designs before they are forced to commit to a budget and start development.

2. Startups and smaller companies

Working with many startups, I find that a significant number of entrepreneurs are focused on the short-term costs rather than the long-term value of their solutions. Even tech-oriented startups are likely to fall into the pattern of 'developing first', typically following an Agile or Iterative method. This is because they are eager to see usable results that can be shown to potential investors or partners and help them clinch much-needed funding. A detailed document containing only research and planning does not make for an impressive presentation to product-hungry investors, after all.

Yet, this becomes a vicious circle of incurring higher costs as time is wasted on inefficient development. There are alternatives to quickly present a great product without heavy investment of time and effort in development. For example, there is a web-based service called InVision where you can build a presentable and visually engaging prototype with no programming required. This process can also contribute to important research requirements for the project (more about this in Chapter 12).

3. MNCs (Multinational Corporations)

With a traditional workflow, typically following the Waterfall model, many MNCs looking to start a custom web or mobile development project fall into a predictable pattern like Mark's.

First, requirements are gathered internally, usually by a project manager without significant hands-on technology experience. While they can interview stakeholders to gather user requirements, they often fall short of asking the right questions to address the technical aspects of those requirements or fail to give stakeholders a clear structure to follow. They also do not consider how the requirements impact each other technically or how they can be merged to improve efficiency.

Based on the requirements, the project manager creates a brief for vendors and expects to receive a detailed estimate back. These non-technical briefs often lack sufficient information about project requirements for vendors to give reliable, accurate estimates. Commoditized vendors will not invest significant time in projects they have not yet won - the cost is simply too high to do that level of research for free. So what the vendor will provide is a ballpark estimate which is only slightly better than an educated guess and usually templated based on past projects. Each vendor will also put forward their platform or technology as the best solution, as MNC project managers are usually not able to independently decide on an appropriate platform as part of the brief.

The client then locks in a fixed budget based on these unreliable ballparks. Typically, there is very little flexibility, if any, to go over this budget. Deadlines are also established and plans made around those deadlines. But all of this is based on a ballpark estimate which was based on an incomplete briefing. It's a bit like buying an unbuilt house for a fixed price based on a sketch someone made on a napkin. And yet, when it comes to custom application development, this is accepted as the norm.

It thus should not come as a surprise when actual cost and time taken overshoot the estimates - usually by a significant amount. The situation is made even worse by the rigid Waterfall model where unexpected changes or delays during development are not prepared for nor mitigated sufficiently.

Changing Tack

The approach I take in this book is mostly Agile but also draws on Waterfall for additional up-front research and risk assessment. I believe that research and planning beforehand can identify and mitigate risks which will help better manage expectations with regards to budget and deadlines. It is equally important not to get stuck in a drawn-out research phase, as tends to happen with the Waterfall approach. Focus on those topics that have the highest chance of disrupting your timeline and budget. Research enough to gain an understanding of the risk and be able to estimate the effort to mitigate or resolve this risk. Keep in mind that you do not need to reinvent the wheel. Consider who might have already researched or worked on something similar and see if the knowledge can be gained through other means - partnerships, or simply purchasing it, for example.

As with Agile, it is essential to recognize that you cannot predict all risks: you must always expect, and budget for, unforeseen events, and be flexible enough to accept changes during development. You will achieve this by quantifying and calculating the risks and likelihood of changes, which will give you margins that you can add to the timeline and estimate. Having margins will help with managing expectations and changes, and unforeseen events can be implemented and managed within these margins. We will go into more detail on this in Chapter 12.

For MNCs, following the Waterfall method means that the development team is not involved until after much of the scoping has been done. This leads to technical decisions either being made by non-technical people or being pushed far too late into the process, resulting in significant changes to the plan after the technical team has reviewed the requirements. On the other hand, startups working with an Agile methodology involve technical team members early on, but with overwhelming expectations of independent feedback and ideation placed on them. This level of involvement also requires the technical team to have a deep understanding of the business, industry and long-term roadmap of the project and business. When working with third party development agencies, in the current market of commoditization, these are unrealistic and unfair expectations.

I have had the best results from projects where the development team was identified early on in the process, and heavily involved in research and technical scoping of the project. However, their involvement was structured and focused on the immediate technical aspects of the project, with the business and long term goals thought out and briefed to them prior to their involvement.

The first part of the project scope (the brief) should give the development team sufficient information to work with and reduce the level of ideation expected from them outside of the immediate technical requirements, while still letting them know the longer term plans for the solution so they can be factored into the architecture and scalability.

This approach is more compatible with MNC workflows and is easier for them to implement than pure Agile. Planning and scoping well will ensure that sufficient margins are added to estimates, as well as managing the development team's expectations early on to ensure they fully understand what is expected of them and are able to estimate appropriately - including sufficient time for consultancy, research and testing.

One more thing of note is that the three methodologies above almost exclusively talk about project requirements, goals and technical features. Rarely do you see any mention of Return On Investment (ROI), business requirements, risk mitigation or other commercial aspects of a project which play an equally important role in this book's approach.

"Listen to stakeholders but give them a clear structure to follow"

3

Kick-Off with a Strategy Session

> **Key Lesson**
> It is important to listen to the stakeholders, but equally important to give them a structure to work within and set business requirements for their requests. In this first stage of the project, you should flag key risks for further research, and gather enough structured information about the project, along with immediate and long term goals, to brief the development team effectively.

The starting point for custom application development projects is a lengthy but structured discussion between all stakeholders to get detailed insights into their goals and requirements for the solution - which is what we call the intended outcome of the project. The focus here is on goals, and how to best achieve them without getting distracted by platform or technology choices. In strategy sessions, my first goal is to educate stakeholders on a better way to approach their project and my reasons for, and experience of, doing this. Often they are already too far ahead, looking at technical specifications and deciding on development matters. This makes them too focused on technical details instead of the big picture - the real goals and users of the solution.

The discussion can be structured from high-level to more specific. Start with the goals: what is your solution trying to achieve? Is it to sell products, increase revenue or perhaps increase productivity? You should find one primary goal and multiple secondary goals, which could include topics such as security or scalability.

Once you know what the solution needs to achieve, you can move on to understanding how the users will contribute to or achieve these goals. This is what we call the workflows. What actions or steps do the users need to go through to achieve one or more of the goals? Consider different types of users and different ways that they might go about reaching the solution's goals. If you are improving existing workflows then you can look at the current pain points and bottlenecks and design a better approach. Workflows should not be technical, so you don't need to consider any specific technologies or how they will be implemented in the final solution. A simple registration workflow could look something like this:

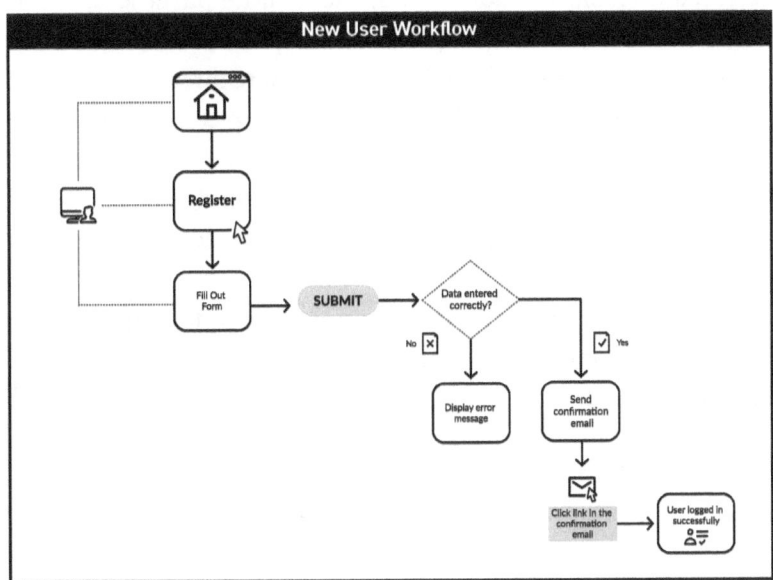

Visualizing a workflow this way usually leads to new insights. Steps that may be missing are easier identified and unclear or inefficient paths can be improved. From the above visual it is easier to notice that an email template and content needs to be created for this particular workflow. This can then be added to the project requirements and included in the estimate.

Once you have the goals and workflows you can move on to the requirements. These are not functional requirements, but rather things that each user wants to have as part of the solution. I recommend using the "User Stories" format from Agile to write out each idea as a requirement. User Stories focus on the human element and are completely 'technology agnostic' - making them easy to read and understand. Even more importantly, user stories include a 'why' element for each requirement. The stakeholder must be able to provide a satisfactory reason to include this requirement. Ideally, the reason should be directly related to the established goals or workflows. Even better would be a specific business case and ROI value (such as productivity or revenue increase) for each requirement - if not, it would serve little purpose to spend time and money developing it. For example, for an eCommerce solution, any features which do not contribute directly to the goal of 'Selling Products' are 'nice to have' and can come later. And if the remaining 'must-have' features can be met by an existing off-the-shelf platform, then that is likely the best option to get started with and the custom platform can come later once the concept has proven itself in the market.

In short, the benefit of the user story format for requirements is a clear overview of what each function does and why it should be implemented.

User Stories format:
As a [type of user], I want [a goal] so that [the reason].

Some examples for an eCommerce platform:

- As a visitor, I want a search to quickly find a specific product that I am looking for so that I don't have to browse through lists of products I am not interested in.
  Get visitors to a product faster = faster sales

- As a visitor, I want to be able to check-out quickly without registering so that I don't have to create a new account for another website.
  Provide the path of least resistance to visitors so they can buy your products fast and have less time to change their mind.

- As an admin, I want to be able to export all sales directly into my accounting software.
  Increases productivity when compared to manual data entry of sales into an accounting system

Note that each requirement focuses on just one action or result. Details about the feature may follow after, but these should be kept to a minimum to avoid cluttering up your list of requirements. The requirements are not meant to be long explanations that expand into multiple sentences. The goal and the reason should be clear but not exhaustive. Breaking requirements down action by action helps to avoid missing anything. A simple rule of thumb: if it does not fit on a sticky note, it is too long. Assumptions are OK at this point; the requirements are only an indication of how the app might work and what you or the stakeholders think that the users might want. We will validate the requirements in Chapter 5 (User Requirements Validation).

Going through the structured steps will result in the general scope of the solution and an idea of what the project needs to achieve and why.

But we don't stop there. The strategy session is also about the business, and we want to identify potential opportunities and obstacles in the target market. For example, integrating payments can be a challenge to certain types of businesses, such as crowd funders and market places, due to the payment providers' terms of service. Before developing anything, make sure to confirm that the payment provider you want to use supports your business model, company size or target market.

Lastly, we want to identify the areas that need researching. The goal is for there to be no major open questions when development starts which could complicate or derail the process. Research can include market research, to validate the concept or specific user requirements, or to gather new requirements that the stakeholders may not have considered. It could include business research, for example if there are conformity issues or data security and privacy implications. It could include technical research: if third-party technologies are required, they may need researching before the developer can be confident of the estimate, or you may need to confirm that any required technologies are practical and available to your target users.

As an option, you could include a technology discussion in the strategy session if some brainstorming is needed on new technologies. For non-technical stakeholders, consulting a Solution Architect or technical consultant can 'fill in the gap' in technical expertise and help navigate through inevitable technology buzzwords to generate realistic and practical ideas. Solution Architects play the role of educating stakeholders on technical opportunities and indicating what is needed to implement their ideas, or describing new technologies which can improve their ideas.

Keep in mind that not all ideas need a custom-built solution and I don't believe in reinventing the wheel. Sometimes, an existing, service-based platform or a self-managed off-the-shelf product may work as-is or be integrated to meet the stakeholder requirements (the deciding factors are discussed in Chapter 8).

At the end, the findings of the strategy session are documented in a format that is understandable to both technical and non-technical people. Each stakeholder needs to be able to understand it, as it serves as an initial roadmap for their project, and it will also be shared with technical vendors to get an initial estimate of time and material cost (see the appendix for the document template).

"A successful idea for a product or service is validated by the market and users, not friends and family"

4

Concept Validation and Competitor Analysis

> **Key Lesson**
> An idea for a project should be based on fact and actual market need, not on assumptions or a perceived value without any evidence. Talk to prospective users and leaders in the industry, and research competitors that may be doing something similar to your idea.

Before embarking on any major project, it is essential to validate the project concept, high-level goals and ROI through research. This will help shape your plan so that it has the maximum chance of success with the target audience.

Market research for new ideas

Research is crucial for market entry and product development in order to:

- define, validate and refine new ideas;
- establish target users; and
- manage or reduce risks.

Market research is a systematic and objective approach to gathering and interpreting market data. In the ideation stage, many assumptions about the market and target audience needs may be made, but these must be validated and refined before planning and committing budgets.

Market research gives a better understanding of target markets and the competitive landscape. Its ultimate aim is to help businesses make informed choices about future decisions, while managing risks and focusing on the most cost-effective and relevant option for their business and budget.

There are a variety of methods that can be used, and knowing how they are undertaken, and their costs and benefits, will be useful in deciding how to conduct market research. The research most relevant to market entry and product development are:

- Concept validation
  validating new ideas with respect to the target market and users

- Competitor analysis
  understanding the benchmark and competitors in the market

- Requirements validation (Chapter 5)
  validating assumed requirements (user stories) with real users and discovering new requirements

Internal Projects

With internal projects, such as an intranet, the concept should be tested with both managers and staff. Looking at competitors is usually less useful in this case. Instead, look at existing Off-The-Shelf (OTS) software products with features similar to what you need before deciding on a custom solution. You should understand what the trade-offs are with OTS products and how they compare with the added cost of custom development. On the other side of that coin, OTS solutions often have recurring license fees or require a license per user. These long-term recurring costs should be compared against the one-time and maintenance cost of a custom project over a period of at least 3 years.

In the following chart we have 2 examples: one is a custom web application with a development cost of $20,000 paid over 4 months of development. The custom site only goes live after this development period. This is followed by a yearly recurring cost of $1000. After 2 years the custom website is upgraded for a one-time cost of $5000.

This is compared against an OTS solution that can go live immediately and has a per-user monthly license cost. For this example we are assuming a cost of $10/month per user with 100 users in the organization: a total of $12,000/year. In the chart we see that the costs of the OTS solution overtake the custom solution in the 2nd year.

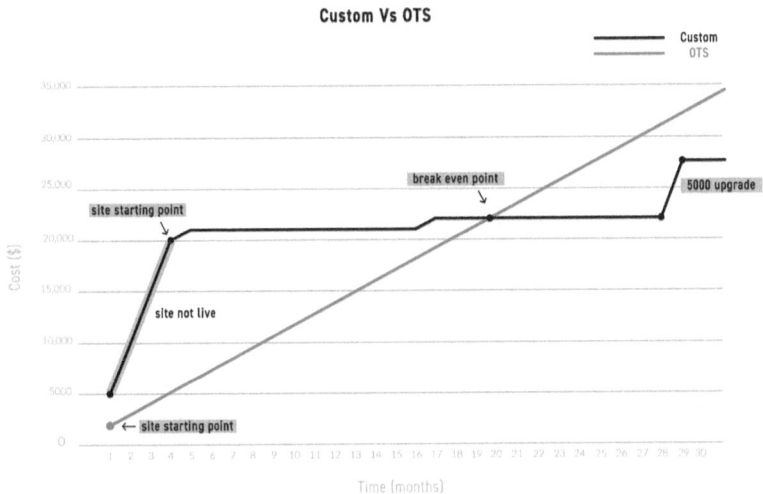

Creating a similar chart for your project and comparing different OTS solutions with different custom development quotes (including a 3-5 year recurring cost) will give you a better understanding of the following:

- the initial buy-in
- the estimated launch date (which can be expanded with revenue projections)
- the financial risk you are initially exposed to (investment vs launch date and expected revenue)
- the long-term cost including recurring fees and planned upgrades
- a fair and detailed comparison between different custom development vendors and off-the-shelf solutions

Outline of market research

With market research there first needs to be a clear aim of what you are trying to achieve, and what information is needed to reach this goal. You would need to know what target markets to test, and what issues or questions you want answered through data collection.

With this focus, methods and content can be tailored to collect and manage the relevant data. A hired market researcher can design and implement research methods, interpret and analyze resulting data, and provide a report of findings and implications to the client, often combined with recommendations on how best to proceed.

The market research report may confirm the idea's viability with information on the target audience's interest and needs, or highlight new issues. This will direct future action on proceeding (or not) with the project as-is or with adjustments to meet the actual target user's needs.

After product launch, regularly planned market research is useful for staying on top of customer needs, market trends and competitors. Your ongoing product or business strategy can then be formed and evolve around facts rather than assumptions.

Concept validation

In concept validation, you may start with a broad target user demographic and narrow it down through your market research. You need to reach out to these people and how you reach out will depend on your demographic: a web survey, an email, letter or, even, inviting a group of them to your office for one-to-one interviews - whatever works best for your project and demographic. The questions you ask depend on your project, but should be largely aimed at finding out more about your target users, their existing needs, and how your app may meet these needs.

Some key questions to consider asking your target group:

- Would you use a service like X?
- Are you currently using anything similar?
- What do you love/hate about that similar service?
- What is a must have feature for a service like X?
- Can we add your email to our invite list so we can give you early access?

Most of these are typical marketing questions with the goal of validating your service. Once it is validated (or if you have already done market research) you can focus on what a user expects from your platform.

The most common method for concept validation is an online survey which can reach many target users in a short amount of time. Survey questions should be designed in order to elicit real answers, without giving away too much of the objective. For example, asking respondents if they would buy your app with a Yes/No answer may not give useful results, as anybody would prefer a free app. However, asking respondents to rank aspects of the app (including pricing), may give a better understanding of the importance of pricing to the target consumers. The same question can be asked in different ways to further verify that the respondents are real and reliable in answering.

Survey design is especially important in engaging respondents, encouraging honest responses and full survey completion. Studies show that long and poorly designed surveys lead to a lower response rate, higher attrition, and lower engagement - this gives biased, unrepresentative samples, increased sampling costs and lower quality answers and results (Comley & Beaumont, 2011).

Your survey should ideally take only 5-10 minutes to complete, and come with a variety of question types (to avoid repetition) and an appealing design. The "Twitter test" suggests that questions (and multiple choice answers) be ideally no longer that 140 characters to ensure it is read.

Finding an adequate sample size is often a problem here for those who undertake market research themselves. Professional market research agencies or consultants have access to a wide database and panel of participants across different regions. A client's own email database allows for control and low to no sampling cost, but may be limited in representing target markets.

Apart from using a third-party market researcher, there is the option of purchasing, via subscription or pay-per-use, online access panels for faster researching, niche targeting and the option of reaching out to non-consumer respondents. However, this becomes costly with the number of regions and users being accessed, and results will still have to be analyzed on your own.

Social media platforms and AWS Mechanical Turk are other options to explore in gathering global participants by yourself. Note, though, that there is no guarantee on the number and quality of participants that are reached.

Key in deciding an appropriate research approach is finding a balance between 'evidence strength' and 'time to execute'. With concept validation you want to get results fast and at minimal effort. With requirements validation the goal is to obtain strong evidence that the solution is the right one.

Competitor analysis

The aim of competitor analysis is to find out who your competitors are, how they are doing in the market and, ultimately, if there is space in the market for your concept. If a target market has established dominant players, it is fair to say that unless your app brings something new or adds value to existing services, it is likely to fail.

A simple keyword Google search of terms related to your concept will bring up most competitors and show the amount of interest in such products. A competitor's webpage will give plenty of information on its business, product features and costs, and main selling points. However, as these are for marketing purposes, it is important to also look at other sources such as user reviews and ratings, or market reports, to accurately understand a competitor's product.

These are simple enough to find on your own, but it can be time-consuming to put together given the number of close and distant competitors and different information relating to them. Identifying key details and analyzing the overall competitor landscape is an important factor in producing a useful report. You should ask what is successful or not in the market, and why, when looking at competitors.

If you are developing an application to support an existing service, and this application has a per-user cost attached to it, you should consider where this cost is going to sit. Does the service you are offering have sufficient margins to cover this cost already, or will you need to improve the efficiency of the service to increase your margins? Will you be able to raise the price of the service and effectively bill the user for that added cost, or will this make you uncompetitive in the market?

[References
Comley, P., & Beaumont, J. (2011). Online market research: Methods, benefits and issues - part 1. Journal of Direct, Data and Digital Marketing Practice, 12(4), 315-327. doi:10.1057/dddmp.2011.8]

"The people using your platform should be your first priority"

5

User Requirements Validation

> **Key Lesson**
> User requirements require a rationale and must be tested with actual users before they are considered valid. Discussions with actual users can also identify new requirements you may not have thought of yet. Organizing these requirements from 'most wanted' to 'least wanted' will help with planning milestones and prioritizing requests during development.

The importance of requirements gathering cannot be understated. Poor requirements can doom your project to failure from the start; proceeding with the project implementation and the basis of incomplete or inadequate information is betting against overwhelming odds. IAG Consulting's report on technology projects[*] finds that poor requirements practices cost companies up to a 60% premium on time and budget.

---

[*] https://www.iag.biz/images/resources/iag business analysis benchmark - full report.pdf

Essential Steps

"In absolute terms, the quality of [user] requirements will dictate the time and cost of the solution." (IAG Business Analysis Benchmark, 2008)

A good user requirement is specific and, most importantly, validated by market research and your business case. Many project owners and development agencies focus on functionality and technology when gathering requirements for their custom web or mobile application. The problem with technology driving the choice of requirements is that it often results in features which are implemented to conform to the chosen technology, instead of the user needs.

The intended users of your application should be your top priority during the requirement gathering phase. Keep in mind that while the CEO and management may provide the overall directions for branding and positioning for the application, input from them on functionality may not match the needs of actual users.

If you build an application without understanding what features/functions the users need, it will result in a poor user experience and you may end up losing them to a competitor. A better approach is to focus on users first. What do the users want to achieve? Once all the user requirements have been established you can make technology choices to best meet those requirements.

User types

Previously, I talked about using the User Stories format to create initial user requirements (Chapter 2).

Recap:
As a [type of user], I want [a goal] so that [their reason].

Who are the users? This is the first question to answer in any good requirements practice. There will be different sets of user types for an app. For example, Mark's eCommerce project would minimally have the 'visitor' and 'customer' users, and the 'admin' user who manages the platform from the admin interface of the application. Less obvious may be a 'marketing' user who wants access to the statistics from the app so they can improve their marketing campaigns; or an 'accountant' user who wants access to all the sales data. Understanding all of the different users and their goals will help you define user requirements clearly and ensure that you are validating the requirements with the right people.

User requirements

Defining user requirements is a continuous process from project discovery to project implementation. The groundwork is laid with assumed user stories from the strategy session, which must then be validated by actual users. It is important to have a strong foundation of validated user requirements for your project to proceed smoothly without major changes during development.

However, user requirements should not be considered final, as there are things you may only discover in later stages, for example new insights based on completed features, changing market needs or new technology trends.

Requirements validation

In order to validate assumed requirements and to identify additional user requirements for the project, interviews or focus group discussions are most often used. These are typically carried out in 1-2 hour sessions with 5-10 people, in an office or a suitably quiet environment.

While online surveys often have preset answers, interviews and focus groups use open-ended questions in order to dig deep into potential user problems and needs. I focus on finding pain points that participants have with current services they use, as this tends to be easier for them to talk about. Then I suggest possible solutions which will lead to requirements. This enables a discussion about what the users really want and how they feel it will work best for them. It will also lead to new insights and suggestions on what can be added or modified to further improve the solution, or what is unnecessary and can be left out to reduce the required budget.

The challenge is finding a representative sample, and even conducting the interview/focus group. Response can be encouraged with monetary incentives, a common tactic for focus groups. If you ran an online survey during concept validation (see Chapter 4), you can consider inviting those who have done the survey or those with interesting responses to the focus group as well. If respondents are not locally situated, you could consider video interviews via one of the many available video chat solutions.

Leading a focus group discussion requires planning and a capable facilitator - professional market researchers may be useful here as they are skilled in asking the right questions. Businesses who do the market research themselves sometimes tend to focus on finding proof for the results they want. The benefit of an objective third party is that they will conduct research in a fair and factual manner, uninfluenced by preferred outcomes, to give an objective analysis and recommendation.

Once you have collected, confirmed and documented all the user stories you will have a fairly strong big-picture view of the entire application. Each user story should be as specific as possible, to ensure that developers know what is expected instead of second-guessing your application's features.

For example, the example user stories from Chapter 3 may become more specific:

- As a visitor, I want a search to quickly show specific products that I am looking for, on one page, as I enter letters into the search field. This means that I only need to type in a minimum number of letters to find what I am looking for.

- As a visitor, I want to be able to go through the entire checkout flow within three minutes so that I can quickly place an order and get back to my other tasks.

- As an admin, I want the system to automatically keep my accounting software synchronized with the confirmed purchases, so that I can minimize any manual bookkeeping work.

With these requirements you can now make informed decisions on the best approach, platform and technologies for your project. These requirements will come in useful again when you have to brief the development team, and to check that the goals of your app are met as development progresses.

Interpreting the results

Apart from designing methods to obtain the right data, the analysis and interpretation of data is also essential to produce relevant and important insights into the market. Objectives of the market research must be answered in this step, and implications for the new product should be highlighted.

With concept validation, competitor analysis and requirements validation, you gain invaluable insights into the target market: defining target/actual user needs, highlighting proven pain points and risks, and identifying market size and competition. This will help assess the viability of a product, and determine its likelihood to sell in target demographics and locations.

Options

1. Self-conducted market research
   Small-scale surveys and focus groups can be run at a low cost to gather information from potential customers, with secondary data collected from publicly available resources. However, this requires you to allocate sufficient time and resources to carry out adequate research - e.g. finding participants for surveys and focus groups. While part of the process can be outsourced by hiring a data collection firm, this still leaves the complexity of managing and analyzing the data and boiling it down to actionable results.

2. Third-party professional market researchers
   Agencies and freelance consultants can be hired to take over the entire market research process, with the benefit of conducting large-scale in-depth research and producing objective, relevant findings. With offices and contacts in different countries, and access to online panels,

professional market researchers are able to reach a larger international audience more effectively.

By understanding the process of market research, you can decide if your team is capable of carrying out small-scale market research, or if hiring a third party would be more cost- and time-effective and give better results.

"Don't spend everything on development, it's hard to succeed without marketing budget."

6

Realistic Approach to Budgeting

> **Key Lesson**
> Avoid setting a fixed budget too early in the project. Ideally, custom application budgets should remain flexible and not fixed until after the Solution Architecture. If you have a fixed budget to start with, then first deduct margins and work with the development team to find a solution that fits within the remaining budget. Most projects will need budget for tasks other than development, so keep marketing, training and other costs in mind when planning your budget.

After conducting user research and establishing their requirements, you will have a better idea of the scope of your project. Before taking the next step, you should have a project estimate and deadline established based on your current projections and funds. This ensures that you do not waste time and effort planning for things that you cannot afford or cannot be completed in time.

It is rarely a case of 'unlimited budget', so knowing what you are willing to spend and when you ideally want the project completed will help you make informed decisions regarding the platform, technologies and your team. For example, if you have a limited budget, a fully custom-built application with all your requirements is unlikely to be possible. Instead, you may be better of starting with a 'Minimum Viable Product (MVP)' and only implement the features that are essential to launch with. For eCommerce projects, where the key goal is to sell products, you should always look for the fastest way to get to market, start selling and grow a user base. Once you have revenue and market share, you can then commit time and resources to develop a more complex custom application.

Every custom application build has risks that will affect the budget and timeline of the project. To help manage expectations, you should assess these risks from the start of the project and have a mitigation plan in place. If you are working with a vendor then you need to first apply the Client-Vendor-Project risk margin (more about this in Chapter 13 - Risk Margin Assessment) to the estimates provided. Then you apply a general margin based on the current phase of the project:

1. Brief and ballpark:
   Add 50% margin
2. Completed Scope research and detailed estimate:
   Add 30% margin
3. Completed interactive wireframes or designs:
   Add 20% margin

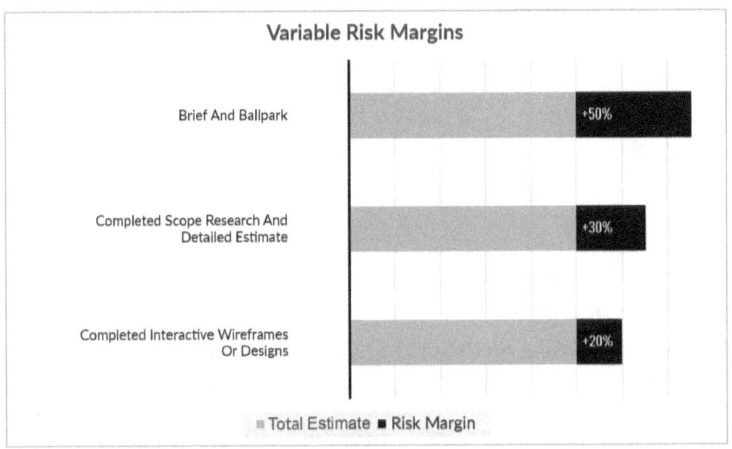

Launch and marketing costs are frequently underestimated. To ensure that you are attracting users to your platform, set aside sufficient marketing budget. A typical eCommerce application will need about the same amount of budget to go towards marketing as towards design and development. For internal projects, budget should be set aside for user documentation and staff training.

If you have a fixed budget to work with, reverse the approach. First deduct an average error margin, and then deduct marketing costs. The remainder is your budget for design and development.

Example breakdown for a public ecommerce app

Your total budget	$100,000
30% for unforeseen changes	$ 30,000
Half of what remains for launch & marketing	$ 35,000
Budget for design & development	**$ 35,000**

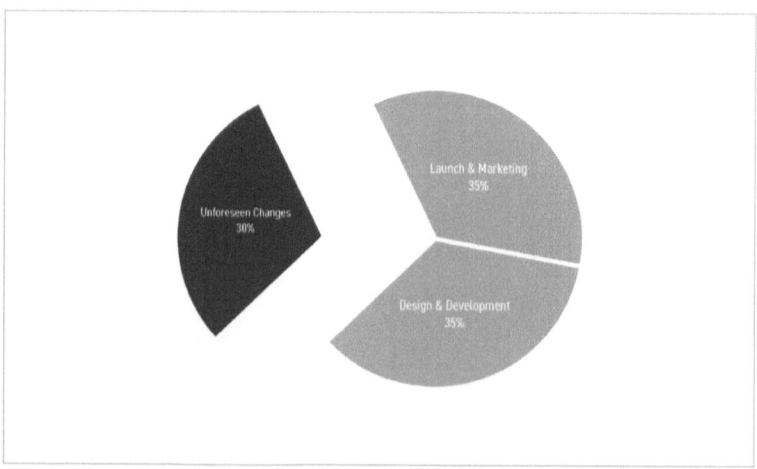

In some countries, you may be able to access government grants for your project. There may be general grants that apply to many industries, or those that are specifically tech or industry-related, which you may be able to bid for. However, grants, while nice to have, should not be a must-have for your project. If your project cannot succeed without a grant then you are in a very dangerous place from a budget perspective. But if there is a grant that you can have access to, you should certainly go after it. That is funding that can support your next phase of growth, after all.

As your project progresses from ideation to development, it will go through three different stages of estimation and value - the ballpark figure, estimate, and final cost.

- Ballpark: This is given after an initial brief or the strategy session, and is, at most an educated guess, based on previous projects and their costs. Your fixed internal budget should not be based on this, as final costs can be significantly different (either more or less), but it should serve as an indication if you are lacking sufficient funding for a particular solution.

- Estimate: This is done during or after a detailed scope or solution architecture, and is based on the vendor's quote or development team's cost, with added risk margins. If researched well, it should serve as an accurate estimate that your internal budget can be based on.

    If design was not done during the scope, then a second estimate may be provided after designs are complete.

- Final cost: The actual final cost of a project after design, development and even marketing.

"'Build it and the users will come' is a very risky, but common, assumption"

7

Planning a Marketing Strategy

> **Key Lesson**
> Don't forget essential parts of your project outside of development. For example, marketing or training costs. When planning your marketing strategy, know your audience and the most appropriate platform on which to target them.

How you will market your project and grow your user base is something that must be planned before any major technology decisions are made, because 'how you sell it' can affect 'how you plan and launch it'. Simply having a website or mobile app does not automatically mean the users will come. You need to find ways to reach out and appeal to them. Researching your competitors or an under-served market will often yield valuable insights as to whether the project will be able to satisfy your user's needs and problems.

Market research targeted at your average user profile will help you craft your marketing campaign and budget. Where is the best place to find and approach your target user? Do your users search for your products and services via search engines? If not, do you engage in active marketing activities through social media, content marketing or community engagements? Amazon book reviews can be an unexpected source for some business cases. Read the reviews on a topic relevant to your business or problem that you are solving. You will see real user feedback, usually both positive and the negative, that give you ideas for ways to reach out to your target market.

Make sure to stick with advertising mediums best suited to your available budget. Traditional platforms such as TV, radio and print tend to be more expensive. For paid Google and social advertising, the cost can be more easily managed as these platforms allow you to shape your campaign according to your budget and goals. Email marketing is also one of the longest available forms of engagement which can be very powerful when used correctly. Aim to provide your recipients with real value and avoid upfront selling, which is usually flagged as spam.

Joining relevant Facebook and LinkedIn groups, writing insightful articles and engaging with members of your online communities can be a great way of generating leads.

For example, if you are creating an eCommerce web app that sells cosmetics, there are thousands following popular YouTube make-up tutorial channels that you can tap into by collaborating with their creators. Forum Q&As such as Quora can also be utilized for this too. Creating marketing content can be very time-consuming but is certainly worth the effort if done correctly.

Business communities are another great avenue for networking. Look for regular meetup groups and events in your area. This gives you access to people who may invest in your app and with whom you can consider forming a partnership. The results are not always immediate, but as you build relationships in a relevant network, there is a higher chance of referrals for your product or service.

You can also get your users to spread the word by rewarding them with exclusive content, discounts or credits for every new user they bring in. This is a proven marketing technique that provides greater credibility to your app as real users are promoting it.

The general rule is that the more it costs, the longer the sales cycle. For optimal results, you should approach users in different phases of the sales cycle, in ways targeted to their current mindset. Are they price shopping, comparing specific products or ready to make a purchase? Consider the best message or call-to-action to put in front of them for each of these phases. When decided on your marketing campaign, get a ballpark estimate from the marketing team (in-house or vendor) to add to your initial budget. Remember, this only gives you an indication, and you should not confirm your budget using ballpark figures.

Part of your marketing strategy should also include tracking your progress with analytics. Whichever platform you pick for your marketing campaign, make sure to set clear goals and milestones. This will help you come up with user acquisition cost and evaluate your success rate, allowing you to end the campaign or repeat it, depending on how well it goes. Tracking marketing goals is typically done with analytics tools which can be embedded into your application. Take time to research the different tools and decide which ones are best suited for your particular application, target market and goals.

If your campaign goal is to increase the number of visitors to 10,000, make sure you are tracking visitors via one of the many web trackers such as Google analytics. If your goal is to sell products, you will also need to make sure you can track sales conversions from individual campaigns. For example, you can configure Google Ads to link to a landing page that allows you to track users while they browse your products and register an account or confirm a purchase.

Not all metrics provided from your campaign are essential to its success. A perfect example is Facebook 'likes': a million likes does not mean they will convert into sales. Be sure to choose the correct metric and information to focus on and in which stages of your overall marketing campaign it should be relevant to. Common metrics to follow are: active users that spend some time in your application and frequently return, users that subscribe themselves to your email list, bounce rate, user churn (inactive accounts for example) and CTR (click through rate) to conversion rate (the number of users signing up or purchasing after clicking through from an ad).

Here are some of the most widely used tools for online marketing and analytics and tracking:

- Google Analytics
  A free and relatively easy to use analytics package. Quick to get started with but has more advanced features for experienced users. Gives you insights as to how many unique visits your site has scored, average visit session, page rankings, visitor demography and much more.

- Google Adwords
  Advertising on the Google network and its search partners.

- Hootsuite
  Analytics and management for social media platforms.

- MailChimp
  A user-friendly email marketing and management tool which allows you to distribute content to your subscribers en-masse.

- Streak
  A Google Chrome plugin that integrates with Gmail to help you track sales-flows and mailings.

- ConvertKit
  Email marketing and tracking. Beyond the email, this tool helps collect email addresses and build automated multi-newsletter workflows.

Analytics will not only help to track and evaluate the success of your marketing campaign, but are crucial in providing information when it comes to design, user experience and content. To learn about your users and improve on your app, you need to monitor key metrics beyond the number of downloads.

While the importance of marketing is clear, I often found that clients forgot to include it in their project scope as they were too focused on planning for development alone. This is also frequently seen in competitor analysis of tech startups, where there are very well-built apps which almost nobody has heard of. Marketing should be planned and budgeted for even before development starts to ensure the success of your app.

"Pick the technology to match the project, then pick the developer to match the technology."

8

Choosing the Right Platform and Technologies

> **Key Lesson**
> Identify the right platform and technology for your project BEFORE you choose your development team. This ensures that the platform and technology is selected based on 'best match for your project', not 'the technology the development team is familiar with'. Look at current and growing technologies, not just tried and trusted ones, to ensure your project is scalable in the future.

Knowing your project goals and budget will help you focus on appropriate platforms and technologies. Ideally, these decisions should be made by an expert in the subject matter who has a broad range of experience across different platforms and technologies. This will ensure that the decision made is the most suitable solution for the project and not based on personal preferences or limited experience in a given technology.

However, this does not mean going straight to a developer with what has been planned so far. The 'trial and error development' route incurs a great risk of wasted time and money. You also risk building something that works for now, but does not scale as your business grows. In the current market, developers are often builders and not business strategists. They are great at building your application as briefed by you but if your brief is missing information and long-term goals then they can only do their best with the information available.

Development agencies also tend to specialize in a particular type of technology or platform, which they will propose for your solution. This does not automatically mean that they are the best match to your project. A third party technology consultant, or in-house technical expert across multiple platforms and areas, is best placed to assess your project and propose the most suitable technical choices. Only then can you be sure you are sourcing for a vendor based on their relevant experiences.

It is recommended to either

1. research and decide this yourself if you have the appropriate experience;
2. find an independent and technology agnostic consultant; or
3. get input from different technology vendors with pros and cons of their proposed platform and technology;

However, if you are working with an in-house development team, your options may be limited.

So what can I do?

Besides having a go-to-market and digital strategy before you build anything, there are also some technical decisions you can make without being a developer. These decisions, which will have a major impact on how your application is developed and by whom, are:

BUDGET
Minimal investment to test the market or bigger investment to make an impression.

SCHEDULE
Launch soon or take your time to build and test something specific to your requirements.

CUSTOMIZATION
Is your idea unique or are their existing solutions that can be built on?

LONG-TERM ROAD MAP
Do you want to keep expanding the current system as you grow (scalable) or build from scratch when you have reached a milestone such as predetermined number of users?

LAUNCH STATE
Will your target audience will accept a beta launch or do you need to debug and fine tune to perfection before going live?

Once you have made your decisions on these factors it will be substantially easier for you to select your implementation type. There are three types, each one suited to different deciding factors but also dependent on availability for your industry and idea.

An existing, service-based platform

These are third party systems that you typically pay a fixed fee per month to use. They offer limited customization and there is no source access. These platforms are usually built on scalable infrastructure and can grow with your business as long as you don't need more or different functionality than they are offering.

Deciding Factors

- Low budget - monthly recurring service cost, on average $50-$200 a month. Initial setup cost is often zero.
- Short timeline - time to go live can be less than a day
- Little customization, usually just logo and theme colours
- Low chance of bugs, this is a fully developed and tested platform
- Usually scalable, most modern web services are built on scalable infrastructure but it's something to check when comparing services.

Benefits

- Low costs so ideal for businesses on a tight budget
- Great for "testing the waters", as a proof of concept to see if there is a market for your product
- Low chance of bugs and no maintenance costs (beyond the recurring service fee)

Drawbacks

- Very limited customization, usually built to serve an average customer base not a specific one.
- There might not be such a platform available for your business goals and target market.
- Monthly recurring service costs and no ownership of product so you are completely dependent on the service provider.
- For internal projects, such platforms may require a license per user; for big business this can get very expensive. Trials should be done with smaller groups before deciding on a company-wide implementation.

Self-managed off-the-shelf solution

Again, a third party system - but this time you get the software to install on your own servers and control the environment. Often you are able to expand/add features with plugins, and many will support developing your own plugins - these include both paid and open source products. The cost for customization will depend on how much you need and if it is done with plugins or new development.

As with any publicly available software, the code and its insecurities are also publicly available. This means that you should update the platform every time an update is released, and you are reliant on the source to provide patches before hackers find them or, at least, as quickly as possible after. The common mistake here is that site owners assume that they are 'not important enough to hack', but hackers run automated scripts to scour the internet looking for vulnerable versions.

Also keep in mind that every time the software is updated you need to review and possibly update all the plugins. If the creators of those plugins don't update them, you might need have them updated yourself or remove the feature entirely to ensure the security of the platform.

Deciding Factors

- Mid-level budget: initial setup cost without customization can be below $1000; with customization anywhere from $5000 to $15,000. Above that, it may be more cost-effective to go with a custom built solution. Recurring cost will be for infrastructure (hosting) and maintenance, which can be $100-500 a month depending on the number of customizations.
- Mid-level timeline: time to go live without customization can be days; with customization 1-2 months.
- Mid-level customization, usually through available templates/plugins. Custom plugins are often also possible but will always be within the constraints of the system.

- Some chance of bugs: the software will usually be quite stable, and the chance of bugs will depending on the amount of customization and plugin compatibility.
- Often not scalable without customization, but this is slowly changing.

Benefits

- Many plugins and design templates are available to build and customize your project easily and quickly.
- Costs can be low if not much customization is needed.
- Usually a lot of documentation and tutorials available: you will be able to find plenty of resources.

Drawbacks

- Must keep the system up to date: this includes all installed templates and plugins, so you may be dependent on many individual developers updating their software or incur substantial maintenance costs.
- Not all such software is scalable: it often requires additional development and maintenance effort and, if the system isn't built for it, this can result in many hours of testing, debugging and a less than optimal system.
- With open-source platforms anyone can see the code and look for vulnerabilities.

Custom built solution

Custom built applications are most appropriate when there is no service or off-the-shelf system available, or when customizing such a system requires a substantial amount of effort. Building a custom application from scratch (or usually based on a framework) will have a far longer timeline and significantly higher cost. Time for testing and debugging is especially underestimated with custom development projects. It is also essential to manage expectations early on: no custom project will be launched without bugs. Even major companies such as Facebook are still finding bugs in their software long after they have launched it. The goal should be to resolve the obvious issues, then launch and pro-actively engage with your users to collect feedback. Try not to get stuck in perfecting the application and wasting many months of valuable exposure. Bugs in an application are not a PR disaster it is how you respond to and manage this process that counts.

Deciding Factors

- High budget: initial cost for custom solutions typically starts at around $15,000 and can run up to $150,000 and beyond depending on your requirements. Recurring costs for infrastructure (hosting) and maintenance can be hundreds or even thousands of dollars depending on the application, number of users, infrastructure design and the agreed scope of the maintenance contract.
- High timeline: typically 3-6 months if you first go live as 'beta'. Going live with a near-perfect system can easily take 9 months or more.
- High customization: system is built to suit your exact requirements and workflows.
- High chance of bugs which will take time to test and debug
- Can (and should) be built to be scalable, both in the application and the infrastructure. Always confirm this with the developer.

Benefits

- Flexibility to build the system exactly as you need it and your target audience expects it.

- Complete ownership of the system and its data, and control to do whatever you want with it - including productizing it for third parties, franchises, etc.
- High quality impression with a platform that is unique and efficient

Drawbacks

- Higher cost, which will increase during development if changes are needed to the original scope.
- Longer time-line, especially for testing the platform across all current devices and browsers.
- Needs a detailed Solution Architecture and research phase beforehand and an experienced project manager or consultant to oversee the build.
- Easy to get stuck perfecting the system which can drag a timeline out for many months.

To summarize

If you want to do a quick test to evaluate if there is a market for your product or service, first see if there is an available service-based platform that is close enough to your needs. This will allow you to evaluate viability without significant investment. If the idea proves fruitful then you can feel more confident investing in a more costly system that meets your exact requirements.

If there is an off-the-shelf product that suits your needs without needing too many plugins or customization you could go with this option. Some investment will be needed, but the solution will usually be quite stable and ready to launch on a short timeline. Be sure to check for scalability of the platform, however, even if your product or service is fairly niche. Websites are global and an influx of visitors on a non-scaling website can slow it down or even crash it.

If you have a very specific idea and there is no service or existing software available, or if you want to build a high-quality and unique platform, a custom solution may be the only choice. This will also be the better option if you plan to productize your solution, if security is high on your requirements or if existing software is not scalable. Be aware and do not underestimate the higher cost and longer timeline, however.

Infrastructure and Programming Languages

This section gets a little bit technical, but an introductory understanding of these terms can help when talking to a development team.

Infrastructure and programming languages for custom web applications and the API (a communication interface to exchange data with third party or mobile applications) of mobile apps will depend on the scope and goals of your project. For example, should you use your own infrastructure, a hosting provider or cloud services? In most cases, a cloud provider such as Amazon Web Services (AWS) or Microsoft Azure will be the most cost-effective option for high-availability infrastructure.

Which programming languages to use will depend on the kind of features and processes your project needs. For heavy algorithmic processes such as report processing, big data and analytics, a good choice would be the languages R or Python. For a lightweight standards-conforming API for your mobile app, node.js is likely the best option. For web applications, you will likely be considering PHP, nodejs, Python or Ruby and their many web frameworks. If you have existing applications and within certain industries, you might be bound to other technologies such as JAVA or .NET. Research or get independent advice on which languages are the best fit for both your project's immediate and long-term goals. Understand the cost differences in development and maintenance on these languages. Understand their risks and how difficult it is to find developers in those languages in your country.

If you are using cloud infrastructure, you should see if it is possible to implement your project as a serverless platform. While it may not be possible for all applications, leveraging cloud services allows you to create complex custom applications without needing to setup and manage servers. This delivers a high level of efficiency with minimal maintenance. It also provides excellent redundancy and fault tolerance in your platform.

When looking into technologies, always consider your long-term goals. For a quick-to-market strategy with minimal cost, you might consider Wordpress, for example. However, you should not forget to factor in the long-term maintenance costs - which can be considerable with customized Wordpress projects. Knowing these costs beforehand can help you calculate if switching to a custom application in a later phase is more cost-effective than starting directly with a custom application for example.

Mobile application development

Many current digital projects involve mobile apps, given their popularity boom in the last decade. However, mobile development can easily be three to four times more expensive than web development. If your project includes a mobile app, you should confirm with some research that there is a clear need for a mobile implementation, ideally together with a clear Return On Investment (ROI). It is also beneficial and generally recommended to create a mobile **web** application first. This will allow you to fine-tune and iterate on the user experience using more affordable web programming languages before replicating the final version as a mobile app.

When developing for mobile, there are two approaches:

The 'PhoneGap' method involves developing the app using web technologies and then packaging it to mimic a normal phone app. These apps can interact with the device's hardware but they will never be as stable or smooth functioning as a native app. This method is great for prototyping and MVPs but is not the recommended approach for most public release apps.

Native development will be more time-consuming and more expensive than 'PhoneGap' apps, but they offer far more in terms of stability and quality. If a mobile app is an essential part of the project and business then this is the preferred approach to develop your app.

With native apps it's important not to fight the platform. Use native elements and design styles, as this will greatly reduce the amount of time needed to develop and test your app compared to building an entirely custom interface. The user experience will also be significantly better as typically mobile users have platform-specific expectations of apps far more than with websites. Keep in mind that if you do both an Android and an iOS app, the two apps will not look exactly alike. Development for the two are also entirely different and generally, it is faster to develop an iOS app before an Android app. The branding will be clearly the same but the interface and controls will differ. This is not a bad thing, because each resulting app will appeal to the users on their intended platforms.

Serverless Architecture

Serverless means an application and infrastructure design that does not include servers that need to be maintained by the client or the developers. The client and developers use a service provided by the cloud vendor while the underlying servers are entirely managed, updated and secured by them. The client pays only for actual use of the service and not the 24/7 cost of keeping servers up and running. This can have a very big impact on monthly hosting costs.

The client and the developers also do not need to spend time on planning scaling, redundancies or managing the operating system or servers which can lead to further cost savings. Recently I helped redesign an existing web application and convert it from a server-hosted design to a serverless cloud design. Their monthly hosting costs went from $2000 to $300 and the application was globally much faster.

Serverless is a bit like staying in a hotel: you pay for your room while you use it and you don't have to worry about the plumbing and electricity, or the beds being changed. A downside is that you would be fully committing to the cloud vendor, and it may be difficult to change providers in the future without having to make significant changes to the application.

An example of a serverless architecture design on AWS is as follows.

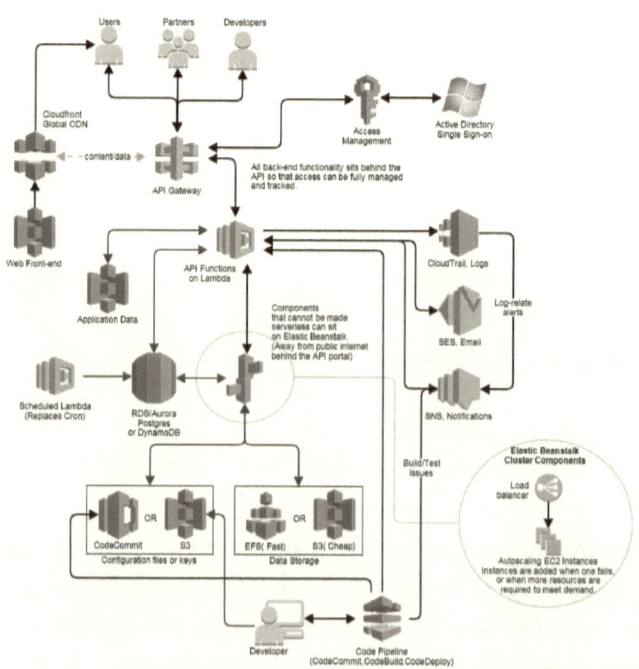

"Ask for long-term estimates when comparing different development teams, as this will help balance the different approaches."

9

Project Team Types Compared

> **Key Lesson**
> If you have a choice between building a team or using a vendor, make sure to do a fair comparison by looking at long term planning, risks and total cost over 3-5 years.

As your project plan comes to life, you will need an implementation team to do the development. When forming a new development team, there are typically four options to choose from, but these are not mutually exclusive. You can mix and match different teams for different parts of the project, depending on what is most suited for that particular part, budget and timeline. I will first cover the pros and cons of each option, before talking about how to form an in-house team (Chapter 9), or evaluate and hire an external vendor (Chapter 10).

Full-Time In-House Staff

Benefits

- More control over the team
- Team is fully dedicated to the project
- Need a manager to communicate between developers and non-technical teams

Costs

- Salary and bonus + government and tax costs + medical or other benefits + work space and services + more
- Long-term overheads as you need to pay full-time staff even when there is no work available for them

Risks

- Sick or vacation leave with no replacement, causing delay in project timelines

Remember

When comparing cost between full-time staff and other options, you should include the additional costs on top of the monthly salary. If you are not from a technical background, make sure to hire a project manager with technical experience who can manage the team and minimise communication errors.

Full-Time In-House Freelancers / Contractors

Benefits

- More control over the team
- Team will be mostly dedicated to the project but there is always the possibility of them working on other projects at the same time
- Compared to dedicated technical staff, there is a higher chance that freelancers will be able to explain and communicate more effectively with non-technical team members and clients. This depends on the experience of the freelancer.

Costs

- Mid- to high- hourly fees + workspace and services

Risks

- Sick or vacation leave with no replacement, causing delay in project timelines
- Other obligations/projects outside of your project may impact timeline and quality (even if technically, your contract stipulates full-time work)
- Not all freelancers are suited to working in teams

Remember

Verify the freelancer's skills and ability to work as a part of a team, and have a backup freelancer on whom you can call in case of issues or in the event of long-term leave. If they are not able to communicate sufficiently with non-technical people or you do not have a technical background, make sure to hire a project manager with technical experience who can manage the team and minimise communication errors.

Local Third-Party Vendors

Benefits

- You do not need to manage the team, only the account manager whom you can meet in person
- Some vendors have redundancies in place for on-leave staff so your project is not affected

Cost

- Mid- to high- hourly fee
- Moderate risk margins

Risks

- Lack of availability due to other projects
- Payment terms (not entirely decided by you)
- Communication issues

Remember

Verify that the vendor is transparent and does adequate planning of a project before getting started. Review payment terms and proposed approach in detail. If you are not a technical person, it is worth finding a third party to evaluate their capabilities before committing. You will also need a technical person to review their code and provide support with briefing your requirements.

Remote Third-Party Vendors

Benefits

- You do not need to manage the team, only the account manager
- Some vendors have redundancies in place for on-leave staff so your project is not affected

Cost

- Low- to mid- hourly fees
- High risk margins

Risks

- May not be able to meet in person
- Lack of availability due to other projects
- Payment terms (not entirely decided by you)
- High risk of communication issues given potential language and time-zone differences

Remember

Verify that the vendor is transparent and does adequate planning for a project before getting started. Review payment terms, testing capabilities, quality assurance guarantees, long-term estimates and proposed approach in detail.

Have a local solution architect or technical project manager to evaluate, brief and manage the vendor in order to provide quality assurance on the deliverables. It is also recommended to have the user-facing interfaces done locally so you can have face time with the designer, and ensure your ideas are clearly conveyed.

What to consider

The choice of any project team type ultimately depends on you, your project requirements, your budget, and how you wish to manage the team. Other things to keep in mind when deciding on a team are:

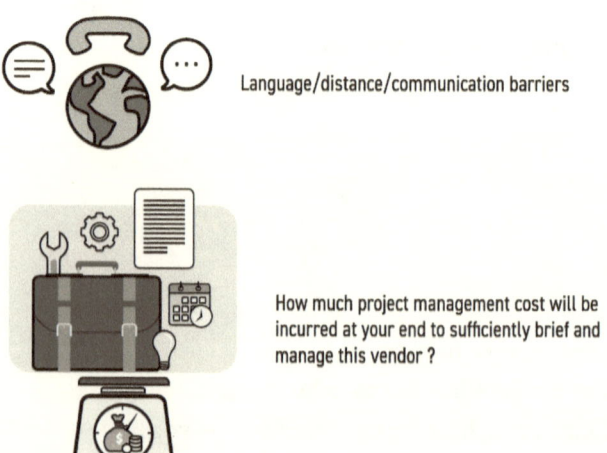

Language/distance/communication barriers

How much project management cost will be incurred at your end to sufficiently brief and manage this vendor ?

Quality expectations and revisions. Different vendors will have different ideas about quality. Research their past projects and look for reviews from past clients. Ask yourself how much time/cost will be incurred at your end to review their code for quality and security and manage change requests and timelines.

Past experience: have they worked on similar projects in the past? This can have a significant impact, certainly where complex or cutting edge requirements are concerned.

The more custom and the bigger the project, the more essential clear communication and availability becomes.

"Custom development needs a team that is agile, scalable and flexible"

10

Recruiting an In-House Team

> **Key Lesson**
> When recruiting a large in-house team, consider a dynamic approach rather than a hierarchical one. Early hires need to be highly experienced across multiple technologies but as the team grows you can focus more on hiring specialists.

If an in-house team is most appropriate for your project or company, you may choose to follow the example of established big development companies in taking a hierarchical approach. This typically leads to teams of followers who are risk-averse, inflexible and difficult to scale. But there is a better way - one embraced by agile start-ups such as Spotify - which involves using dynamic teams assembled from a pool of specialists for each project.

This more dynamic approach to engineering teams involves not hiring managers, but instead appointing solution architects or 'full stack' developers - highly experienced 'all-rounders', with the skills to turn a brief project description into a detailed project plan. They independently undertake scoping, research and planning for the project, and identify the users, appropriate technologies, rough ballpark and key research points or questions to ask. All of this can be documented in a project pitch for the key stakeholders to approve.

The Research Team

Once the pitch is approved, the solution architect will assemble their research team from a pool of available talent. A typical research team would have the following members:

1. Copywriter

While they are not engineers and usually do not have any hands-on development experience, they are able to understand technical terms and explain them to non technical people. They are also capable researchers for non-technical matters, such as market research and user interviews. It is their role to take all decisions and insights from the team and explain them coherently in the solution architecture document.

2. Business Consultant

The business consultant provides insights and undertakes research on all business matters, including finances, legal and compliance. They can add appropriate risk margins to estimates and calculate operational and other non-development costs. They can also research and write business cases for each requirement and ensure that there is an ROI - this can be productivity, revenue, efficiency, and so on.

3. One or more Technical Specialists

These team members have extensive experience and deep knowledge of the technologies identified by the solution architect for the project. They are able to turn user requirements into technical specifications, design infrastructure and databases, and create detailed and accurate estimates for all tasks.

4. Designer / UX specialist

A designer is essential for any project with user-facing interfaces. They can provide user experience insights during scoping and, once the requirements are known, they are tasked with creating interactive wireframes for every interface of the project. These are essentially complete designs but without any branding (colours, specific icon designs, etc). This allows stakeholders and users to focus entirely on the functional aspects as proposed, instead of being distracted by colours and other design details.

Solution Architecture

Once the research team has been assembled, it researches and documents the solution architecture in detail. The goal of this document is to cover every angle of the project, answer every question, mitigate every risk and leave nothing to chance. The project estimate included in this document should be accurate to within 10%. Collaboration is key, with each team member contributing their insights and knowledge where appropriate in the document. The Copywriter will format and write the content consistently and in a way that is understandable to all readers, regardless of their technical capability.

Once complete, the Solution Architecture can be presented to the stakeholders for their approval. Budget can be assigned and any buy-ins are also secured at this point. Projects can also be considered 'not recommended'. If the research points out that there is insufficient ROI or challenges that cannot be met, the project may not continue. Valuable lessons are still learned and documented for future reference. Importantly, with this approach, almost all projects that would have failed during development are identified before development even starts, saving significant cost and time.

Implementation Team

After the project has been approved based on the solution architecture, the technical specialists from the research team will then assemble their implementation teams from a pool of developers, testers, freelancers and vendors. The specialists will be heavily involved with their team and fulfill the role of facilitators. The solution architect will be the product owner and update stakeholders as needed. The implementation team will need to be briefed (I will discuss this further in the next chapter), and then you can get a ballpark estimate of time taken and cost for the known requirements.

It is generally recommended to pair each developer with a reviewer. These are second developers that review the main developer's code on a weekly basis. This has three benefits:

1. You always have a backup developer who is fully familiar with the code.
2. You have a second pair of eyes on the deliverables to ensure security, quality and efficiency in the code and to ensure all code is fully documented and easy to understand.
3. The main developer has a sparring partner to bounce ideas off.

Testers should also be involved with development from the very start and not only once development has been completed. Automated testing through unit tests and tools is also a must.

The research team is dissolved once implementation starts, but the solution architect will continue with high-level monitoring of the project throughout implementation. They will be available for support for any major changes and can bring in the research team members again as needed. It is also their responsibility to ensure the solution architecture documentation stays relevant to the project, with any changes being updated right away. This document should be versioned so all changes can be tracked for evaluation later.

Completion

After final testing, the solution architect, perhaps with support from a copywriter, will turn the solution architecture documentation into the project document: a guide or manual to the project and all its parts. This may also include technical documentation extracted from the code. An evaluation document will be created that lists the tracked changes made to the solution architecture document throughout implementation. This can be used by the solution architect and the facilitator to gain a better understanding of the changes and to make improvements to knowledge or workflows to help minimize such changes in future projects.

When the solution architect is happy with the presentation of the project they will deliver it to the stakeholders. The solution architect will be involved in any training and feedback sessions to gather change requests and plan a new phase of the project. Together with the facilitator, they will make recommendations for a maintenance team for day-to-day support of the project, and the implementation team will be dissolved.

Pros and Cons

Con: Benched staff

There is a high risk of staff being benched if they are too specialized. Certainly at the beginning of the hiring process it is important to hire versatile staff capable of working different roles to ensure they can be kept busy across different projects. For example, the copywriter role can initially be filled by the solution architect, and they may also be able to fill the business or technical roles. Another option, not ideal but easier to implement in early days, would be to have a team comprising existing staff on loan from other departments for the duration of the project. Later, as the team scales, increasingly specialized staff can be hired into the project team pool.

Pro: Agile, flexible and scalable

The nature of the structure means team members can be added from both internal and external sources, allowing teams to scale easily with specialist freelancers or vendors for peaks in project loads, and steadily grow by hiring into roles with a proven frequent need. All new staff will require some onboarding and training to help them acclimatize to this new way of working.

Con: Difficult to find the right solution architects

Many solution architects are specialized in a particular technology, but for this structure it is essential that they are technology agnostic. They need to be able to identify the best technology for the project without any bias and then work with a specialist in that technology to work out the details. With the right guidance and structure in place, appropriate candidates can be trained to become the right type of solution architect.

Pro: Team communication, shared responsibility and risk

All team members must be able to communicate effectively and bring something valuable to the table in their assigned role. They are all responsible for delivering the project goals and each member's insights are valued equally.

Team members who only seek to follow, are not team players, are overly risk averse or have insufficient knowledge in their assigned role will be quickly identified through their lack of participation in project groups. They can be approached for a one on one discussion to find out what support they need in order to find their place in a team.

Con: Friend-policies

While team members must certainly be able to get along it is more important that team member selection is based on their experience and knowledge being relevant to the project, and not only because they are friends with another member of the group.

Pro: No fixed managers but equal team members

Helps prevent politics and managers monopolizing the best staff. Teams are created specifically for a project and are then disbanded once the project has met its goals. All team members are selected based on being most effective for the needs of that particular project.

Hybrid Option

Early in your hiring phase you may not be able to grow a large enough pool of specialists to work dynamically. Instead, you can start with permanent staff making up your team's core members who are key to your project. And on a project-base, you can bring in freelancers or vendors to provide their services during the phases that require more manpower or specific skills. This mix also aids with the onboarding process as the permanent staff can support new freelancers, and it helps with long-term planning as some freelancers may be open to a full-time position when it is available.

"Keep your management time, communication and quality assurance costs in mind when comparing vendors"

11

Hiring Third-Party Vendors

> **Key Lesson**
> Talk to your prospective vendors and make your expectations clear. Don't be afraid to ask questions, and request for research and consultancy time as part of the proposal. This becomes worth it in the long run, as it reduces delays and complications.

Before hiring a vendor, you will first have to write a project brief for vendors before they can provide any estimates. A specific, detailed and technical brief will get the most accurate estimates as developers know clearly what you want and how to go about doing it.

A non-technical person creating project briefs would focus on goals (rather than technical specifications), which is a good thing to start with. However, briefing only goals to a development team will not give them enough information to reach a realistic estimate of time and costs involved for your project. It is equivalent to asking an architect to estimate the cost of building a house - many assumptions such as the choice of materials have to be made if not enough details are given.

A good technical brief will consist of the following:

1. Technology agnostic user goals tested with actual users and backed up by a business case, or with a clear reason that supports one of the project goals or workflows. This means that the user goal should be specified in terms of **what the user wants to achieve**, and **not technical specifications**.

2. Technical specifications and functions derived from the user goals and workflows, an indication of ideal platform or technology to use for implementation, plus an indication of areas of research. All research needs to be completed before the technical specification can be considered complete.

3. Interface wireframes for every page of the application. Each one should reference the user goals and technical specifications to ensure a consistent brief between the functional and the visual.

To get the best possible estimates, you must ask the right questions and manage both your own and the vendor's expectations. But which questions should you ask, and how should you ask them, to ensure that you get consistent estimates from multiple vendors?

There are two approaches to writing a brief. If you have an experienced technical partner to support you, then you can provide a full detailed brief. This will ensure that the ballparks provided, while not perfect, are as accurate as possible. A detailed brief includes doing internal research, speaking to each stakeholder, asking the right technical and strategic questions, and gathering as much information as possible before consolidating it into a single detailed project brief. It also involves understanding technologies and platforms and picking the best one for your project before a development team is selected.

If stakeholders have different requirements for the same feature, then those need to be resolved between the parties before being finalized in the brief. A ballpark based on a detailed brief should be reasonably accurate - typically to within 30% of the final bill for the specified requirements.

If you do not have a technical background or support, you will need to select a vendor and do a more detailed brief in the next stage with them. The initial estimate will not be dependable in this case.

When you work with the vendor on a more detailed brief and estimate, keep this and the following chapters in mind so you can ensure a structured and sufficiently detailed approach to get the best possible estimate before committing to implementation.

Viewpoints

A great briefing includes different viewpoints on the project within the business. For example, a finance person may have different goals and requirements from the project than a salesperson. It is important to understand the needs and goals of each and every stakeholder and to find consensus in the final brief. Factors you should consider and understand are:

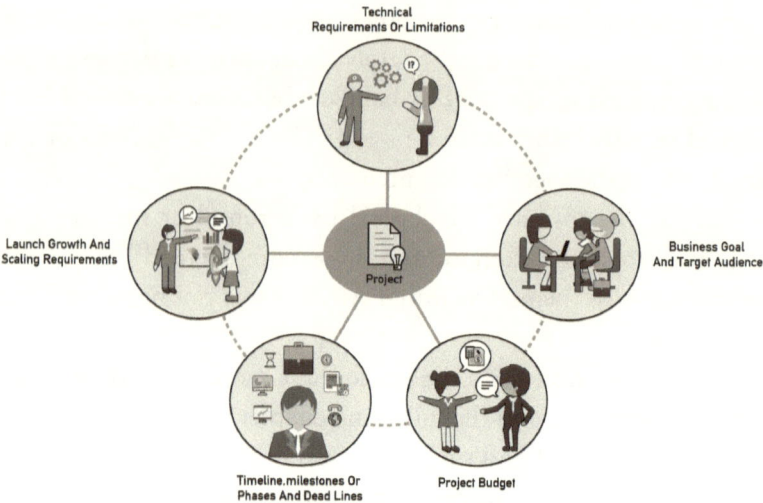

For small businesses without staff, the entrepreneur may have all of the above information but should try to have additional input such as an external consultant or someone from your target audience who can help provide viewpoints you may have not considered. A single point of view is never a good thing when it comes to briefing a complex custom solution.

Too many decision-making stakeholders should be avoided as it will result in delays and a messy, incoherent brief and project. When it comes down to two stakeholders wanting something different, there needs to be one person who can swiftly make the final call on how it will be implemented.

Feature Estimation

For a development team to be able to provide effective estimates it is essential that they have sufficient information. Validated user stories are a good basis. These clearly convey what a user expects from the system. They function both as requirements as well as test cases once development has completed. But user stories alone are insufficient. If you have technical experience or a technical partner, you should be able to break the user stories down into specific tasks. If this is not within your capabilities, then you can communicate this expectation to the development team as part of their estimation efforts.

User stories should first be split into three sections:

1. Function
   What functionality will this user story provide? Consider calculations, retrieving/storing data or processing a file, for example.

2. Data
   What data is involved in this user story? Specific files such as user uploads or database fields, for example.

3. Design
   Which part of this user story will be visible to the user, and what will it look like?

Once the sections have been identified, one or more tasks for each section can be written out for the development team to estimate. When estimating how long tasks will take, the best approach is to specify either 1, 2, 3, 5, 8 or 13 hours per task. The rationale being that the bigger the task, the harder it is to accurately estimate the time required to achieve it. With the above, we increment each step after 3 with an increasingly larger number to ensure padding is included.

Any task that requires more than a day (8 hours) of development should be broken down into smaller tasks. The 13 hour option is available for some limited exceptions. Ask your development team to follow this approach and you will get more realistic estimates. It will also help with consistency when comparing estimates from multiple development teams.

Budget Range

Budget is a bit of a polarizing matter when it comes to briefings. Do you include your budget range or not? From the vendor's perspective there are, depending on their capabilities, thousands of ways to implement a given project - each with different budget and timeline requirements, technical constraints and level of quality. Most vendors will want to implement the best solution because it will be high quality, properly tested and fully scalable, but these are also the most expensive solutions and may not suit your budget.

Stating your budget range will manage the expectations of the vendor and they will be able to propose a solution that best fits your available budget. This may be a solution that uses a design template instead of a custom design service, or an existing CMS product instead of custom development, both of which can make a difference in the thousands of dollars. Just make sure that no corners are cut when it comes to research, security and testing and remember to keep aside some budget for margins and additional testing or fine-tuning later.

If you really have no idea about your budget or it's a strictly kept secret, then ask the vendor to ballpark three versions: the cheapest they can do, a middle option and a high-quality option. Ensure that they clarify the differences between each solution with the pros and cons. This will enable you to fairly compare the different vendors on a similar level of quality for each project.

Fixed Price

Fixed price requests come from a position of mistrust. Like Mark, many businesses have bad experiences on past custom development projects. Even when they have not bad experiences themselves there is a certain amount of prejudice due to stories and statistics from the industry. The reaction to this is that businesses ask for fixed price in the belief that this will mitigate their risks.

Fixed price is the wrong solution for custom development projects because nobody benefits from it. It might reduce the cost risk to the client but it creates many new risks in other aspects of the project. Expectations are poorly managed and quality can suffer when corners are cut. A project will always change, so if a vendor is providing a project at fixed price, there are three steps they can take to reduce their own risk exposure.

- They can add risk margins to their project estimate. Without doing thorough technical research, this will only be an educated guess. So they either under-margin and end up going over budget, or they over-margin and client pays more than they needed to.

- If they go over budget, then the vendor may opt to cut corners so they can reduce their internal cost on the project. Typically, security, testing and quality assurance are the first to be reduced.

- Alternatively, the vendor might opt to carry the additional cost themselves and lose their profit margins. But this is bad for both morale and the business relationship, and it can be disastrous for the business if it happens too frequently.

Paying vendors based on actual hours worked is a fair solution as the vendor is appropriately compensated for their work and the client only pays for work completed. But for this to work, it is essential that the project be scoped and planned in sufficient detail, estimates appropriately margined and risks mitigated as far as possible.

Other Topics

The brief should include the type of implementation for the project (see Chapter 8 on platform and technology choices) as this is key to establishing the size and general scope of the project. Note that the type can heavily influence the budget.

Also include a description of the main expected features, your key business goals of the project, the target audience, the platform your project is intended for and, for web applications, any specific browsers you want to support or a general year ("all browsers from 2015 onwards", for example). If the vendor is to provide design services you should also reference two or three websites or apps with a design style similar to that which you are expecting.

Communicate Expectations

To manage expectations, it needs to be clear to both parties what is expected from the briefing and the estimate. Vendors should not be expected to spend a significant amount of time on researching and working on a detailed estimate before the project has been awarded to them. This is a very big risk to vendors as such detailed estimates typically include valuable consultancy and ideation. But you, as the prospect client, should also be able to form a fact-based opinion of each vendor and their budget proposal for the project. To satisfy both of these requirements you can follow a two stage approach:

Stage 1 - Ballpark: a quick proposal which includes a profile and ballpark cost estimate. This is to be provided free by each vendor. A vendor should not need more than a day or two to write up a ballpark based on a given brief. It's important to note that a ballpark should NOT be used to establish a final budget within the business as this is very likely to change during the next stage.

The vendor should also include an estimate for Stage 2 as this will require significant effort on their part.

Stage 2 - Solution Architecture: a fully documented project plan which includes research, detailed cost estimate, timeline proposal and more. This will be the first paid stage of the project after you have selected a vendor. The accuracy of the included estimate should be sufficient to establish an internal budget, but still be sure to include some margins for new features that are requested during development.

Profile

Besides a proposal based on your brief, you should also request a profile from the vendor whereby they answer at least the following questions:

- What programming languages do they specialize in?
  It is in line with the platform and language identified for your project?

- What infrastructure do they use?
  Cloud or standard hosting services? they should include a ballpark of the expected costs.

- Are their solutions scalable, both for the code and the infrastructure?
  Should include an explanation of how they achieve scalability in code. For the infrastructure you will want to know if scaling is automatic or manual.

- How do they manage development and live systems?

Will they be developing in your live application after it launches or will they have a separate development environment and a change-publish approach?

- What are their testing/QA processes?
  Internal by developers, internal testing specialists, external testing specialists or a combination of multiple methods. Also enquire if they can offer on-site testing to test the application at your premises or that of the end user.

- What are their backup and staff redundancy policies and measures?
  If their developer is sick does the project stop, do they do versioning and/or backups of the code, media, content store and databases

- Can they provide an example of a back-end interface they have developed?
  Does it look intuitive, something you and the users would be happy using on a day-to-day basis?

- Do they provide full server and source access?
  At which point in the project life cycle is it provided? Right away, after each payment, or not until the end of the project?

- What is their policy on bugs?
  Is debugging within the specified scope, limited or to be paid per hour? Is there any warranty period or do they offer an SLA for long-term monitoring, testing and debugging?

- What are their payment terms?
  Everything up front, monthly or in stages, pending your approval of a milestone, for example

- For mobile apps, do they develop native apps or 'PhoneGap' style apps?
  If PhoneGap for a live app, what is their reasoning?

There will likely be more questions specific to your industry or project so think carefully about what would be red flags or requirements for your particular situation.

Stage 1: Ballpark and profile evaluation

After receiving all replies you can evaluate the vendors. Look for red flags to quickly rule out vendors that are not suitable or higher risk than others.

- Any specific requirements or questions that were ignored, and clarify why they were ignored - for example, do they not have the skillset for this?

- Repeatedly late for meetings, conference calls or the ballpark deadline

- Vendors suggesting a project type different to that which you requested: clarify with them first to ask why, as they could have a good reason - although lacking the skills or experience to implement the preferred type is not one.

- No contract/vendor agreement: vendors without at least a basic contract are also likely to fall short in other areas of account and project management

- Vendors proposing features purely for the sake of the it, without any thought to the business goals (upselling): all features, and especially complex and expensive ones, should be justified with a strong business case.

An orange flag is if the vendor does not have a solution architect or a senior engineer with both technical and commercial capabilities that can fulfil this role. If you have your own technical support, this is less important; but it indicates that this vendor is likely to follow the blueprints and implement features exactly as requested without any thought for the overall strategy or long-term goals of your business. Not always a bad thing, but certainly something to keep in mind.

Make sure to review the vendor's contract. Is it heavily biased towards the vendor or the client, or is it balanced? Are there clauses that are vague or at odds with their pitch, how they answered the profile questions or what they have said during meetings or phone calls? The contract should also allow you to cancel the project after the initial research phase if the detailed estimate/timeline turns out to far exceed your budget. Note that you are still expected to pay their time spent on the research but you should be free to discontinue the project at that point.

A good vendor will tell you if certain features are a bad idea, will be honest and transparent and will make an effort to have a long-term business relationship with you because they know their service will live up to, or even exceed, your expectations.

A bad vendor will implement all features without question and regardless of their added value; they will be secretive and evasive about their experience and existing client details, contractual obligations and pricing; and they will focus on getting as much work approved and signed for in the first step, because they know they might not be considered for a second step.

Review vendor

Once you have made your decision, make sure to select a backup vendor for redundancy. In the case of turnover or long-term leave, your project may be delayed and even put on hold if nobody is able to take over. A backup vendor, who should be specialized in the same programming language or skill set as the selected vendor to ensure compatibility, serves as a contingency for such situations.

Instead of having a backup vendor doing nothing, let them serve as a review vendor. The review vendor acts as a second developer who reviews the main developer's code on a weekly basis. Thus, the backup developer becomes fully familiar with the code and can take over smoothly in any contingency. The presence of a reviewer also improves the security, quality and efficiency of the delivered code, and ensures that all code is fully documented and easy for other developers to understand. Keep in mind that for this to work, you will need to have access to your source code early in the process - so ensure that this is covered in the contract and payment terms.

"Always expect unforeseen events that will increase cost and time"

12

Risk Margin Assessment

> **Key Lesson**
> Risk margins are essential to managing expectations but are often underestimated. Instead of having a generic percentage you add to all projects, look at the key challenges of a project, the vendor, and your own behaviour to calculate a risk margin appropriate to the situation.

Besides comparing the skills, portfolio and experience of freelancers and vendors, you will compare prices. This is not as simple as comparing and calculating the differences between their different hour or day rates. After getting the vendor estimate, you need to factor in risk margins which will be different per vendor type, as well as add your own costs for managing them or hiring someone to do so.

Managing expectations can make or break your experience during the project. It is better to think your project will cost 200k when it ends up costing 150k, than expecting it to cost 100k but it ends up costing 150k. The final cost is still the same, but in the first example, you are far better prepared for any 'what-ifs' and end up pleasantly surprised. The additional 50k that was planned can then go towards additional features. In the second example, expectations are not met which will lead to frustration and missed deadlines.

The fact that developers do not always give an estimate with adequate risk margins is due to the commoditized industry in which they operate, which forces them to compete on price. Lowering their price involves overly-optimistic estimates of time and cost without sufficient risk margin assessment. The general perception is, "This is what it will cost if there are no changes during development and you communicated everything precisely," which is entirely true, but not practical. It is essential for you to add your own risk margins that are both realistic and calculated for this specific project.

Using key attributes specific to the client, project and vendor, you can calculate margins for your project. Below is a list of key factors needed to calculate a simplified risk margin. These were identified as having the biggest impact on project timelines from over a decade of data from multiple projects across various industries, company sizes and vendors.

The Project

In general, the longer the project, the more risk it incurs. However, there is no straight correlation between timeline and risk. An urgent project with a tight deadline is always significantly riskier due to the pressure and overlapping workflows. Dependencies on third parties adds risk as well as the number of unknowns or research items at the time of estimation.

The Vendor

The team's experience together and the experience of their lead developer in general and with similar types of projects are key risk indicators. Their location with respect to the client can affect communication and increase risk. Vendors that challenge their clients' ideas tend to get better results as do vendors with well thought out development and testing workflows (also called DevOps). A vendor that takes sufficient time to do some research before development starts is a good indication of quality. Lastly, as with most things when it comes to cost: you get what you pay for.

The Client

Different types of clients have very different expectations when it comes to custom application development. The client's experience in custom application development as well as with the specific vendor can have a big impact on project timelines, expectations and communication. Clients who tend to pivot or experiment a lot add significant risk to a project, as do multiple decision makers. Availability of a client has an impact on communication and catching issues before they spiral out of control.

The Project

Project Duration

Total estimated number of workdays that this project will require as provided by the vendor. Note: this should be actual days worked by the different developers and what their estimate is based on, not necessarily the same as the project timeline.

Project Brief

The level of detail briefed to the vendor before they provided their estimate.

- ☐ Brief description
- ☐ Non-technical project manager brief
- ☐ Detailed technical brief and user stories
- ☐ Full Solution Architecture

Design State

The level that the designs were at when you briefed the vendor. If the project does not require any design, select the last option.

- ☐ No design information available
- ☐ References to existing websites or apps or partial wireframes
- ☐ Approved wireframes for all pages or partial graphic designs
- ☐ Approved full graphic designs for all pages

Urgency

How urgent is this project? Do you have a specific launch date or is it flexible? If you have a hard deadline, did the developer indicate that this is achievable or will overtime and additional resources be required?

- ☐ None / flexible deadline
- ☐ Hard deadline but sufficient time
- ☐ Hard deadline and insufficient time, or only sufficient with overtime

Dependencies

Total number of third party dependencies outside the client and the development vendor that this project requires. This includes products, services, SDKs and APIs provided by partners or vendors, marketing agencies providing content, freelance copywriters or designers, etc.

Research Items

Total number of items that still require any research. Include third party APIs and tools that the vendor has limited or no experience with.

The Vendor

Vendor Experience
Total number of years that the company and team has been active. For freelancers, this is their total years of relevant work experience.

Developer Experience
Total years of relevant experience of the most senior developer on the project. For freelancers, this will be the same as Vendor Experience.

Similar Projects
Number of projects similar to this one that the vendor has worked on. This can include projects for the same industry or a similar category of project (e.g. social, collaboration, eCommerce or intranet).

Location
Where the vendor is located relative to the client. If they are not local, to what extent they have a local presence that can have face-to-face meetings with the client?

- Different country to client with no local presence
- Different country to client but with a local project manager.
- Different country to client but with a local project manager and technical person

Interaction
How interactive is the vendor with the client? Do they simply implement as requested or is there a high level of discussion and feedback involved? Do they behave like an implementer focused on creating a project, or a partner with the success of the project and the client's ROI in mind?

- Vendor estimates and implements without much discussion
- Vendor initiates discussion to clarify the requirements, and may offer alternatives for some requirements
- Vendor requires a brainstorming or strategy session to discuss the project in detail, and many different approaches to the requirements are discussed before the best is identified

The Vendor

Testing Capability

The topmost level of testing service that the vendor can offer. Note: this is what the vendor is able to offer reflecting on their capabilities, not necessarily what was included within the project scope.

- Developers test their own code
- Dedicated testing/QA team
- Dedicated testing/QA team and unit tests
- Dedicated testing/QA team, unit tests and Test Driven

Approach

What type of approach does the vendor propose for the project? Do they just get started with development or do they take some time to fully plan out and design the project before development starts?

- Vendor gets started with development right away, iteration happens throughout
- Vendor will debrief the client and provide a high level proposed approach to the project before development starts
- Vendor will do research and create a detailed project scope and technical blueprints before development starts

Day Rate

The rate that the vendor charges for one day of work (or their hour rate multiplied by 8). If you want to use the online risk calculator you should convert the currency to Singapore Dollar.

The Client

Type of client

What type of client is involved in this project and how are they funded? Do they have sufficient resources of their own or are they dependent on third parties?

- Agency managing the project for a different end-client
- Large corporate or multinational
- Self-funded startup or a startup depending on government grants
- SME, existing profitable business
- Startup that is already funded by investors or with significant own capital - sufficient for the entire app and marketing

Project Experience

The number of custom development projects this client has been involved with in the past, either as a client or representative of a client.

Disruptiveness	How disruptive is the client likely to be during development? Will they request major changes to the scope once they see the interface in action or will they be able to lock everything down before development ☐ Highly likely to make major changes to the scope and goals of the project during development ☐ Changes very likely, but without major implications to the project structure ☐ Unlikely to make changes once development starts or, if they do, they will be minor ☐ Guaranteed not to make changes once development starts
Avaliability	How available is the client for meetings and updates during development? Will they only have time for major milestone reviews or are they readily on call for any question the vendor might have? ☐ Not available for review/feedback until the end of the project ☐ Available for key milestone presentations only ☐ Available at frequent but planned intervals during the project ☐ Readily available whenever needed
Who is managing the project on the client side?	The person managing can have a big influence on the project flow and results, and has the responsibility of translating requirements between the two parties and managing their expectations. ☐ Staff or owner with little or no development experience ☐ Staff or owner with a minimum of five years of development experience ☐ External party or partner with significant development experience (not the vendor)

Once you have collected all of the information, you can fill out a free risk assessment calculator at https://binarythinktank.com/carma-calc.html to retrieve a risk margin indication that you can add to your project. The calculator, while a simplified version, is based on over a decade of data from custom web and mobile application projects across different industries, company sizes and development teams.

Examples

The following are two project examples using this CARMA (Custom Application Risk Margin Assessment) Calculator. These examples illustrate how different attributes affect the calculated risk margins.

Example 1

A successful SME assigns an experienced project manager to scope and manage a 3-month project. This manager has several years of technical and management experience with past custom projects. The manager, who is familiar with the essential steps of solution architecture, works with a local vendor. A decision on vendor is made based on capability and approach rather than only price. The solution architecture phase has ended with all research successfully completed and results documented. The manager is now calculating a risk margin to apply to the final detailed implementation estimate from the vendor.

- Client
  - Type: SME
  - Project Experience: 5
  - Disruptiveness: Unlikely to make changes once development starts, any changes will be minor.
  - Decision Makers: 1
  - Availability: Readily available whenever needed
  - Project Manager: Staff with a minimum of 5 years development experience.

- Project
  - Duration: 60 days
  - Project Brief: Full Solution Architecture
  - Design State: Approved wireframes

- Urgency: None
- Dependencies: 3
- Research Items: 0

- Vendor
  - Vendor Experience: 10
  - Developer Experience: 10
  - Similar Projects: 3
  - Location: Fully local vendor
  - Interaction: Vendor initiates discussion to clarify the requirements and may offer alternatives for some requirements.
  - Testing Capability: Dedicated testing/QA team and unit tests
  - Approach: Vendor will do research and create detailed project scope and technical blueprints before development starts
  - Day Rate: 600

- Risk Scores:
  - Client: 18/100
  - Project: 11/100
  - Vendor: 12/100

- Recommended Risk Margin: +17%
  - What this means for the timeline:
    - Estimate: 60 days
    - Margined: 70.2 days

  - What this means for the budget:
    - Estimate: $36,000
    - Margined: $42,120

Total Implementation Budget

To calculate the budget requirements for implementation, you must remember to factor in project management time and add this to the margined vendor estimate.

- The margined timeline is 70.2 days.
- The client's management time is calculated to cost $350 per day.
- For a project with full solution architecture you need about 20% project management time (one day a week).

Based on this, the project management budget is approximately $5000.

This makes the total implementation budget approximately $47,120.

Example 2

Two first-time entrepreneurs with no technical experience embark on a three month project that they aim to fully manage themselves. Both have equal say and decision making power on the project requirements. Unfamiliar with the essential steps of solution architecture, they plan to iterate along the way and so pick a vendor based on price alone as they do not see the value of research and extensive scoping. Similarly, the vendor is less experienced and is focussed almost entirely on developing the requirements and not on research or planning.

- Client
    - Type: Self-funded startup
    - Project Experience: 0
    - Disruptiveness: Highly likely to make major changes to the scope and goals of the project during development.

- Decision Makers: 2
- Availability: Readily available whenever needed
- Project Manager: Owner with little or no development experience

* Project
  - Duration: 60 days
  - Project Brief: Brief Description
  - Design State: References to existing websites or apps
  - Urgency: None
  - Dependencies: 3
  - Research Items: 5

* Vendor
  - Vendor Experience: 3
  - Developer Experience: 5
  - Similar Projects: 0
  - Location: Different country to client with no local presence
  - Interaction: Vendor estimates and implements without much discussion
  - Testing Capability: Developers test their own code
  - Approach: Vendor gets started with development right away, iteration happens throughout.
  - Day Rate: 300

* Risk Scores:
  - Client: 88/100
  - Project: 61/100
  - Vendor: 100/100

- Recommended Risk Margin: 105%
  - What this means for the timeline:
    - Estimate: 60 days
    - Margined: 123 days

  - What this means for the budget:
    - Estimate: $18,000
    - Margined: £36,900

Total Implementation Budget

To calculate the budget requirements for implementation, you must remember to factor in project management time and add this to the margined vendor estimate.

- The margined timeline is 123 days.
- The owners' time is calculated to cost $350 per day.
- For an iteratively approached project you need at least two days a week or 40% project management time.

Based on this, the project management budget is approximately $17,220.

This makes the total implementation budget approximately $54,120.

Summary

Comparing the two examples, the effect of spending time appropriately scoping and planning a project quickly becomes apparent. In example 2, the margined vendor estimate exceeds the initial vendor estimate, but is still lower than the margined vendor estimate in example 1. That is, until you factor in the costs of managing the project on the client side which results in example 2 significantly exceeding its budget and deadline.

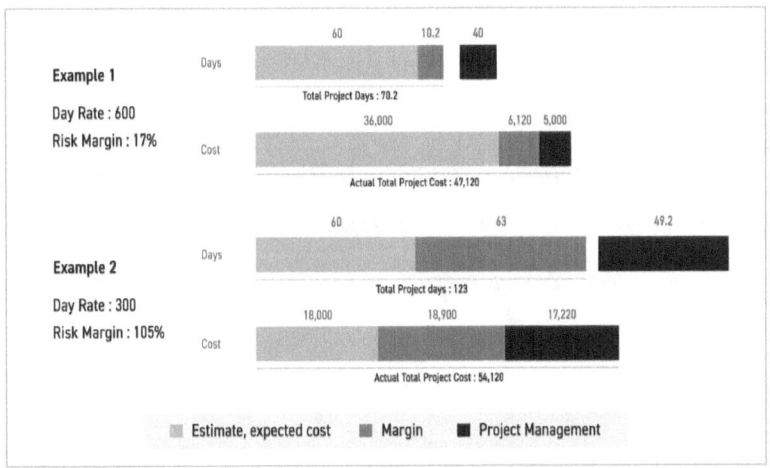

Tech entrepreneurs tend to be quick to brush aside the project management cost. They claim that they are happy to put this time into the project and it shouldn't be considered a project cost. Being involved in the process is commendable, but entrepreneurs should be primarily focused on their budding business - acquiring users/customers, selling their product/service, attracting investors and promoting the brand. The more time they spend on project management, the less time they are spending on building a successful business.

"Assumptions and unknowns with a high chance of affecting timeline and budget should be researched before development starts"

13

Technical Research & Wireframing

> **Key Lesson**
> Researching unknowns will help you with managing expectations on the project and ensure that estimates from vendors are more fact- than assumption-based. Be careful not to get 'stuck in research', however. Keep it agile and fast by identifying those unknowns that can have the biggest impact to time and budget, and research those first.

Up to this point, I have talked about finding the right development team to work with. This is stage one in a three-stage process of working with your development team:

1. Stage 1 - Sourcing
   a. Identify the platform and technology most suited to your project. Include this in your brief.
   b. Assemble a development team or source a development vendor with experience in this platform and technology.
   c. Get a ballpark estimate for the project from the team.

2. Stage 2 - Research
   a. Establish the research items and questions. Discuss with the team to find any that you may have missed.

Obtain an estimate from the team to research and document these.
   b. Team completes the research and answers all identified questions.
   c. Team provides a more precise estimate for implementing the entire project.

3. Stage 3 - Implementation
   a. Team develops the project.

The research stage is the first paid stage for your chosen development team, and will be very helpful when writing the Solution Architecture document. Before any development starts, it is essential to identify as many unknowns as possible and research those that are most likely to affect the project timeline. Every feature request needs to be assessed. What questions can you ask about its implementation? Most of these questions can be answered by the stakeholders or yourself. Any that cannot be answered may need technical research by the team.

Take the the Simple Storage Service (S3) offered by Amazon Web Services for example. It can store files online, and if needed for your project, the brief could simply state 'Use S3 for file storage'. But this leaves too much room for error and misunderstanding. So, as part of the technical research scope, the following questions can be identified for this feature:

- The files
    - What type of files are we storing, how small and how large can they be?
    - What actions do we need to take with files? Add, remove, download, etc.? Do we only need download, or also stream or display inline (videos, audio and/or images)?

- How many files do we expect, and how frequently will we be adding and downloading the files?
- How secure do the files need to be? Should they be encrypted, for example, or can they be publicly accessible?
- Do we need to keep the files forever or for a fixed duration? Can we archive older files? Do we need versioning for the files?
- Will we be storing files with original file names? Could these filenames include special characters?

- The service
  - Is S3 an appropriate service to store this type and size of file and does it meet the security requirements?
  - What would be an appropriate workflow and service for handling archiving of older data?
  - What will S3 cost for the expected number of files and transactions?

- Prototype
  - How do we store a file on S3?
  - How do we retrieve a file from a public S3 store? And from a private S3 store?
  - How do we delete a file from S3?
  - How do we archive a file?

You can see that even a feature initially assumed to be as simple as 'storing files', has many questions that can be asked. If the questions are not identified beforehand, with the effort for researching and answering these included in the estimate, you will face budget creep as they are identified later on in the project or, worse yet, implemented wrongly and have to be redone.

Other types of research can include:

Researching the viability of a technology in the current market. While there are always new or trending technologies around (such as Virtual Reality, as I write), the market and average user is not always ready for them. Their devices might not be compatible or they may require specialist hardware that is not yet generally available or too cost-prohibitive for your intended user group.

Using third-party tools to help reduce development time. For example, if your project involves augmented reality, there is a plethora of third-party tools (also called libraries or SDKs) available that can give your project a base set of features to build upon. This can significantly reduce the amount of time you need for development. However, each tool will have its own pros and cons that should be researched and compared before a decision is made. The exact features offered by each tool, any known bugs, how active is development, is support available, do you get the source code, and what are the licensing costs: are all important questions to ask when deciding on the most appropriate tool for your project.

At the same time as technical research, a similar approach can be adopted for creating visual interfaces for the project:

1. Stage 1 - Sourcing
    a. Select a designer most suited to the type of project and get a ballpark. With designers, experience is key. Most importantly, the designer must have interactive design experience and not only print experience. Within interactive design there are also many sub-categories of experience:
        i. creative marketing design

      ii. public web application, such as eCommerce where user experience and digital marketing are important
      iii. internal intranet application, where user experience and automation are most relevant
      iv. mobile design, which has some unique requirements that differ from web application design

2. Stage 2 - Wireframes
   a. Designer should start with static wireframes for the most important pages. These are basically black and white images of the interfaces. There should be no branding, and no colours involved to keep the focus entirely on the functionality. For web applications, the designer should create a desktop, tablet and mobile version of each wireframe.
   b. Once you are happy with the key pages, the designer can proceed to create wireframes for every page of the project. Nothing should be left out. After the wireframes are made, the designer can create an interactive experience with them using software such as InVision. This will give you a functional experience of the application by seeing every page (in black and white) and being able to click buttons and navigate through the application.
   c. When this experience has been fine-tuned and approved, any changes made to the scope of the project can be updated in your project document and discussed with the development team for any impact on the estimate and timeline.

3. Stage 3 - Design
    a. Using the wireframes as a base, the designer can now fill in the colours and branding elements to complete your designs. This could be done by a different designer who is more experienced with your branding but less with the technicalities of strong UX. It is important however, to ensure that no bright colours are applied to unimportant elements in the design. Final designs can also be assembled in InVision as an interactive preview, allowing you to test the designs with users to ensure they are being led into the right workflows and do not get confused anywhere.

Stage 2 can be done at the same time as technical research. Stage 3 can actually be done during development as it is unlikely that there will be any functional changes.

The interactive wireframe and final design previews make excellent demos in some cases. They enable you to put together something a user or investor can play with, without having to invest substantially in any development. Using InVision, you can also emulate the user experience of an app without having to code anything. Iterating in this software contributes to technical research, and can help obtain far more accurate estimates for development.

"Think first; scope and research the key challenges before development starts."

14

Solution Architecture

> **Key Lesson**
> Waterfall spends too much time researching, Agile not enough. Find a balance that works for your situation, but avoid starting development when there are still too many unknowns in key requirements. Document your findings in a way that is understandable to both technical and non-technical team members to ensure communication and transparency across the board. Collaborate with specialists where possible.

When building a house, you do not go directly to a building company and have them start laying the foundation without any planning. You first have an architect draw up a blueprint of the house. The same is true for custom application development - you should research, design, plan, estimate and document your project before any developers start working on it.

Design and Research

Cost and budgeting

Construction and Testing

Project Launch!

It is equally as important not to get 'lost' in research. Identify those areas that are of the highest risk to your budget and timeline and collaborate with specialists to get research done efficiently. This process is called Solution Architecture (SA) and it is what this book aims to help you achieve.

"Projects with an SA show a 19% **decrease** in overrun."
– *Business Value of Solution Architecture*, 2009.
   R. Slot, Capgemini.
   G Dedene and R. Maes, University of Amsterdam.

While the steps are listed chronologically, writing Solution Architecture documentation is rarely a linear process. It involves writing a draft and initial solutions, researching, then going back and rewriting things. The entire document is basically in flux with changes happening across all sections, until it stabilizes and becomes a consistent, clear guide to building the project: a document of problems with the best possible solutions.

In SA, decisions and proposals are backed up by years of experience or facts from research and prototypes. Solutions to problems should be the most efficient option - not just for the feature itself but for the application as a whole; not just technically the best solution but also the best solution from the business and user perspective; not just for the first version but also for a long-term roadmap. The completed product is your project plan covering user requirements, research, prototyping, designs, risk and opportunity analysis and much more; but it is also your project reference and documentation after it has been launched.

Following the essential steps will help you in creating your own SA document, help you understand what to expect if you approach consultants and larger agencies for this service or help you manage vendors to improve relationships and project results. The goal of an SA is not a 'be all and end all' project brief, as there will always be unforeseen events. Instead, it is to cover the key requirements, risks and challenges from a technical **and** a business perspective.

Designs can be part of the Solution Architecture - certainly, work-flows and wireframes for the main interfaces should be included, but full graphic designs for the project can help convey the requirements more clearly and help reduce miscommunication and revisions later in the project.

Other topics to consider in the Solution Architecture include: backup and security policies, user training, service level agreement for ongoing support from the vendor, business model and revenue streams and opportunities for partnerships. For in-house projects: the opportunity for productization, near-future technologies that could impact the project, available grants, and innovation or tech awards.

Once your project is documented, you will be ready to start developing it, knowing that you took steps to find and mitigate risks beforehand and manage expectations of all involved parties.

Epilogue

Try reading through Mark's story again. Does the first half of the story still seem like he is doing everything right or can you identify where he went wrong and what you would do differently? Similarly, look back on projects you may have managed that did not turn out well. Knowing what you have learned from this book, can you identify areas you could have improved in that project?

The steps in this book are all about scoping and preparing for a project. I do not go into managing the development phase but this may be the subject of a second book one day! However, I can pass on the following tips:

- If the project starts going wrong, try not to get emotional. Focus on facts. Projects frequently miss deadlines and budgets and, while frustrating, acting frustrated will not resolve anything and can even make the situation worse. Many developers are introvert to some extent, and frustration, blame and threats accomplish very little with them. Focus on the positive aspects of the project. Remember also that the visible part of a given solution, the part that you see and are finding bugs in, only represents about 10% of the entire project. If you only see issues in the visible parts then that likely means that at least 90% of the project is working as intended.

- Keep track of the project without micro managing. Establish a clear and consistent update schedule whereby the development team delivers updates (good and bad!).

All progress should be transparent, and communication should be open and honest. I can recommend a project management tool called Trello (.com) as it is easy to use and great for collaborative project management.

- Ensure the development team is versioning the code and that you have access to the source code early on. Avoid 'hostage' situations with one party withholding payment and the other withholding source code. Nobody wins in this situation. I have always gotten far better results from developers where there was a relationship of trust. Where I paid them for each month of estimated work in full up-front and had immediate code access while they were developing it. This allows for timely reviews of code and facilitates a more effective partnership between the client and vendor.

- Don't rush change requests. When a new request comes in, follow the same procedure as scoping a project. Research the request, verify it as needed, answer any questions and understand how it will impact the application as a whole. Wireframe it if there are visual aspects, and implement the request only once this has been completed.

- Try not to get lost in details. Rarely does an application need to be 100% perfect to launch; if you chase this ideal you will very likely drag the project out and miss deadlines. Get the application launched as soon as it is stable, and work on non-essential issues in following update cycles together with user feedback.

If you have any questions please feel free to get in touch via https://binarythinktank.com.

Appendix

Scoping Template

The following list of topics can be used as a reference for things to consider when scoping your digital project. The topics are picked based on the amount of impact this knowledge can have on your timeline or budget. They should be considered flexible and adaptable. If topics are not relevant to your project you can leave them out; if there are additional topics you feel are important, then add them in. For each topic, consider the fastest method to get the information, to avoid getting stuck in a lengthy research phase. As a general rule of thumb, completing the project document or solution architecture should not take more than 10-15% of the total project timeline.

1. Information Gathering

This section is aimed at collecting existing information. The focus should be on users and workflows, not on technology.

1.1. Project Summary

A one-paragraph description of the project, its primary goal and users. New readers should quickly understand what this project is about from this summary.

1.2. Benefit and Value

All projects need to have clear and stated benefits. The proposed solution and deliverables should align with the project goals and strategy. Also consider what is the selling point of this solution for your customers/users? Why would they pay for it? What value does it give them or what problem does it solve better than any existing solution that may be available? Think critically and be prepared to validate any assumptions with market research.

1.3. Kick-off Meeting Debrief

A brainstorming session for a new solution, or a discussion with a client to better understand their needs and gain a deeper understanding of the project. It's important to have a structure and format for this meeting. Recommend to start with goals – what is the purpose of the solution. There can be primary and secondary goals. Then identify and map the workflows – what steps should users go through to achieve those goals. Are there existing workflows we are seeking to improve, or are these entirely new workflows? Then move on to requirements. These should be structured and follow some minimal rules. Where will this requirement be in the solution, and who is it for? Most importantly, every requirement needs to have a reason. Why are we including this requirement? Does it contribute to one of the goals or improve a workflow? Try to avoid talking about specific technologies and implementations. Focus on the user and their needs, and later we will find a technology that best matches those requirements. This topic should have a summary of the discussion – sufficiently detailed to give new team members the same information and insights. Note that the requirements will be outlined in a separate topic below so they do not need to be listed here.

1.4. Initial Considerations

This section is intended for your own thoughts on the project. You may have new insights or identify new risks while writing out the kick-off meeting debrief, for example. You can also include concerns, high level risk assessment and additional areas for research. Try not to focus entirely on the project: also consider the stakeholders – do you have any concerns or see any opportunities there?

1.5. Target Users and Regions

This entire stage is generally more focused on users and this specific topic is the highlight of that. Here you can document who those users or user groups are. This is a fairly standard market research process. The idea is that you have a clear idea of a humanized user of the system, it can help better understand them and scope accordingly. If this project is about product development, then describe the first client – be precise so the business developer knows where to start looking for opportunities.

1.6. Research Topics

List out all topics that should be researched before the project starts. Technical research topics should be included but do not need technical details as these will be found under the next chapter. Include any questions you have about requirements or users, as well as the risks you don't yet know how to mitigate. Also consider non-technical aspects of the project, such as market research or legal/regulatory concerns.

1.7. Team Members

Describe the different members involved in this project.
To be considered:

- Description of stakeholders, availability, experience
- External vendors. Summary of each vendor and their rates, strengths and weaknesses
- Designers, content managers, marketeers
- Quality assurance and testing
- Long term maintenance vendor or staff
- If there are plans to hire staff for the project then any recommendations for hiring, what to look for, experience, average market rates, etc.

1.8. Competitor Analysis

Essential topic for new concepts. Which businesses are doing this already or are similar? How does this concept differ from them and how to win their clients over? This section should be a summary based on research. For internal projects, instead of looking at business competitors we can look at existing software/SAAS solutions offering something similar. How does the scope of the project compare to what they are already offering.

1.9. User Stories

User stories are an agile method of requirements notation. Identify the interface or area, followed by the type of user. Then add each requirement in the format of a goal followed by a reason. It is OK to have assumptions at this point; they will be validated in the next stage.

[Interface or area] / [User Type]

- I want [a goal]
  So that [their reason]

- I want [a goal]
  So that [their reason]

2. Project Research

This section is about validating assumptions and answering all the questions and research topics you identified during Information Gathering. For the sake of speed, make sure to consider any team members or external specialists that could provide answers more efficiently than researching everything yourself.

2.1. Target User Research

2.1.1. Concept Validation

Describe the means used to validate the concept. Reference the survey, for example. If you did not do the research, then indicate the research required here. If a third party did the research, then summarize their goals and results here.

2.1.2. Requirements Validation

Describe the means used to validate the precise requirements for the project: reference the interview questions for a focus group, for example. If you did not do the research then indicate the research required here. If a third party did the research, then summarize their approach here, amending the headers as needed.

2.1.3. Summary and Recommendations

Summarize recommendations based on the completed research. If no research was done, then leave this topic out or emphasize the need for research before the project starts.

2.2. Business Processes

Describe the different business processes related to this project. Include workflow visuals. This should focus on workflows on the stakeholder business side, not the users.

2.3. Content and Interaction

2.3.1. Sitemap

Short summary showing the sitemap of the project's interface(s). Multiple summaries if there are different interfaces, including how the different interfaces relate to each other. This is a non-technical page-based description focused on how a user would experience browsing through the application.

2.3.2. Required Content

Describe the content that is required from the stakeholders or content partner for this project. List each item in order of priority and include the following information for each item:

- Description of content item
- Date by which it is required
- Current status (Pending, Reviewing, Complete)
- Person responsible (name and contact information)
- Last contact date/time
- Any notes

2.3.3. User Workflows

Short summary and step by step visuals showing the actions taken by different users for key sections of the project across multiple interfaces. Make sure to consider things that can go wrong and include paths for these and how to recover from them. For example: login -> password rejected -> display invalid authentication message -> return to login. Focus on how a user experiences the workflow rather than the technical specifics and backend actions.

2.4. Design

2.4.1. UX Research

Any research done or recommended for the User Experience aspects of the project. Quotes from existing third party research that are relevant. May also include recommendations on what should be researched, A-B testing or user interaction monitoring, for example.

2.4.2. Design Brief

The brief that is to be provided to the designer for this project. Should include expected milestones, design references, style and branding availability and choices. Can also include internal notes such as 'must be local', and budget limitations, but these need to be clearly marked as 'internal only'.

2.4.3. Analysis

Description of the design, analysis of the different sections and any changes that were made during the design that need to be updated in the SA and with the development team.

2.5. Technical Research and Prototyping

2.5.1. Goals and Requirements

Describe all items of technical research in detail. Include technical specifics, consider this a brief for the development team on what they need to research and what is expected in terms of results (deliverables) and timeline. If a prototype is required for this project then it should be described here. What are we trying to prove or answer with the prototype? What are the expected results and how are we going to go about it? Should this prototype be usable for demos or anything else after our research has completed, or is it an internal-only developer prototype?

2.5.2. Results and Recommendations

Describe the results of the research and prototype. What challenges were faced in creating it? How were they resolved? What was proven or disproven? What did we learn?

2.6. Policies

2.6.1. Backups and Redundancies

What are the backup requirements? How much data-loss is acceptable (RPO) and how fast should the platform be restored in the event of failure (RTO)? Multi-region considerations. Redundancy goals.

2.6.2. Information Security

What data do we have and should it be encrypted? Specific tables, files, stores and/or attributes. Which level of encryption and can it be decrypted by the system or user input only? Simple passphrase encryption or public/private key?

2.6.3. Access Security

User access levels to the dev/production infrastructure, servers, code base, application interfaces. Type of access, password requirements, change password requirements, access duration, server roles and service access, ip restrictions.

2.7. Risk Analysis

2.7.1. Business and Concept Risks

Assess potential risks to the business model or the concept itself. Competitors, location or target audience risks, third party dependency risks, funding or innovation risks, fraud and social engineering risks, staff/vendor risks.

2.7.2. Technical Risks

Assess potential technical risks, data security, target-potential for hackers, technology availability (high-end technology requirements for example limit the potential user base), browser or platform risks (should older IE versions be supported?), chance of dependent technologies becoming obsolete.

3. Architecture

This is where it gets technical and typically you would do this with a technology consultant and the vendor. It is best to have a second opinion here which is why I recommend an independent technology consultant, but you could also use a second development vendor to support you.

3.1. High-Level Structure

A high level breakdown of the major sections of the project. For example, here you can indicate if there is an API, website, admin or a mobile app, and if it's hosted locally or in the cloud.

This can be non-technical as it is intended to give a high level understanding of the platform and architecture to management and non-technical stakeholders.

3.2. Interfaces

Drill down in more detail into the individual interfaces. Admin - Website - Background processing, for example. Establish the main points for each interface: is it user-facing? Is it running heavy algorithms or data processing? etc. This can contain technical details and requirements. In some ways this will mirror the sitemap but needs to contain significantly more technical detail.

3.3. Code Workflows

Describe how data flows through the system and is handled by different sections. Some overlap with user flows but should be on a more technical detail level. Will also include background processes that are not included in user flows. Use visuals to better convey the design of the workflows.

3.4. Background Processes

Describe all background processes of the system: anything that will be built into the application, including backups, unless handled by third party backup software. Should include but also distinguish between cron startup and timed background processes and asynchronous processes called by the application.

3.5. Technology and Language Recommendations

Which technologies/platforms are most relevant for this project? iOS, Android, Windows, Web, etc. And which programming languages are best suited for different parts of the project?

3.6. Infrastructure and Services

3.6.1. Goals and Requirements

Where will this project be hosted? What are the infrastructure requirements in terms of processing power, number of expected users or processes? Platform-specific services to be used for which purpose, which database-type to use and why, etc.

3.6.2. Design

Infrastructure design. Include development and production environments. Development and production environments and workflows.

3.7. Code Base

3.7.1. Framework(s)

Which framework(s) will be used? Angular for front-end, nodejs or php framework for backend, etc. Provide information about the framework, especially license, frequency of updates, complexity in upgrading to a new version in the future, etc.

3.7.2. SDKs and Dependencies

Any SDKs and third party dependencies that you are going to rely on. Facebook SDK for example, or any nodeJS modules or Angular plugins. For dependencies, indicate failover options and risks.

3.7.3. Third Party APIs

Typically only include APIs that are extensively used and that the platform relies on, such as passbook providers, banking systems, etc. If only using Facebook for likes or shares, for example, it can be mentioned above in SDKs and left out of this section.

3.7.4. Application Structure Breakdown

This application structure breakdown will depend on the type of project and platform. For API, list out all methods with their path, method, description, params, response. For a mobile app or static website it might follow a Page or Class breakdown. The point is to go into technical detail of what is to be programmed. This is the blueprint and is what the developer team will be following, so it needs to be detailed enough to avoid misunderstandings. UML designs are optional, certainly for mobile or heavily abstracted class structures.

3.8. Database Design

Like the application structure breakdown, this needs to go into detail on the database schematics. First describe the different database types/services involved and the reason for using those. Then list out each database with its name, type, id logic, read/write speeds, indexes and attributes. Each attribute should include name, type and description. Connections between different databases (tables) should also be made clear, certainly for relational databases. Graphics are recommended in this case.

3.9. Storage, CDN and Other Services

Specifics on storage if needed (AWS S3 for example). If a CDN will be used, for which sections, expire settings, etc. Any other miscellaneous services not mentioned so far.

4. Launch and Follow-up

This section is about the go-to-market strategy. You should consider things such as training or marketing and factor this into your budget requirements.

4.1. Go-Live Procedure

The approach to going live with this project. Consider any data that needs to be synchronized, setup the production environment, update links, etc. Also consider training, marketing or other related activities.

4.2. Support / SLA Recommendation

Any requirement or recommendation on a service level agreement or ongoing support. Internal or with a vendor. If hiring staff is a consideration for maintenance, then provide the job description and requirements.

4.3. Evaluation

Post-project evaluation. Include major changes to the planned approach, key lessons learned and evaluation of budget and timeline expectations vs actual. List new risks that were discovered during or after implementation and changes that will have an impact on policy or approach in future projects.

5. Timeline and Estimate

Initially this will be a ballpark but, as you validate assumptions and complete research, this should get more and more precise. Remember to calculate and add the risk margins.

5.1. Project Phases

How this project will be broken down into phases: MVP/Beta/Phase 1 production/Phase 2 etc. This should match the budget availability or specific milestones, such as number of users at which point a phase 2 will be required to accommodate the growing user base.

5.2. Timelines and Dependencies

A detailed breakdown of the timeline. This does not need to cover all future phases and should focus on the immediate timeline up to first production launch. Set clear milestones and dates for client feedback/review. It should follow 2 or 4 week sprints with, ideally, something presentable at the end of each sprint. For dependencies, it should clearly reflect which items need to be completed before a next item can start, where relevant.

5.3. Cost Estimate

Detailed cost estimate for the project. Keep in mind that the items noted should be understandable by non-technical persons. As such, focus on user requirements or groups of requirements, not technical deliverables. Be sure to clearly state development, testing, monitoring/fine-tuning costs. Include recommendation on margin for risk mitigation, total or per section. Any recurring costs should be listed separately: hosting/service costs, for example, or third party API costs (per request/month/etc.).

5.4. Payment Schedule

When working with a development vendor, establish the expected payment schedule: milestones or monthly, and what is the expected invoice total for each month or milestone. For long-term recurring fees, such as hosting or SLA, how frequently they will be invoiced and whether a fixed cost or dependent on the activity during that period.

www.ingramcontent.com/pod-product-compliance
Lightning Source LLC
Chambersburg PA
CBHW031050180526
45163CB00002BA/772